CRYSTALS AND CHAKRAS FOR BEGINNERS

The Power of Crystals and Healing Stones! Discovering Crystals' Hidden Power! The Guide to Expand Mind Power, Enhance Psychic Awareness, Increasing your Spiritual Energy

BY

Cassian Byrd

TABLE OF CONTENTS

COPYRIGHTS

This book

"CRYSTALS AND CHAKRAS FOR BEGINNERS: The Power of Crystals and Healing Stones! Discovering Crystals' Hidden Power! The Guide to Expand Mind Power, Enhance Psychic Awareness, Increasing your Spiritual Energy."

Written by Cassian Byrd

This Document aims to provide precise and reliable details on this subject and the problem under discussion.

The product has marketed on the assumption that no officially approved bookkeeping or publishing house provides other available funds.

Where a legal or qualified guide is required, a person must have the right to participate in the field.

A statement of principle, which is a subcommittee of the American Bar Association, a committee of publishers and Associations and approved. A copy, reproduction, or distribution of parts of this text, in electronic or written form, is not permitted.

The recording of this Document is strictly prohibited, and retention of this text is only with the written permission of the publisher and all Liberties authorized.

The information provided here is correct and reliable, as any lack of attention or other means resulting from the misuse or use of the procedures, procedures, or instructions contained therein is the total, and absolute obligation of the user addressed.

The author is not obliged, directly or indirectly, to assume civil or civil liability for any restoration, damage, or loss resulting from the data collected here. The respective authors retain all copyrights not kept by the publisher.

The information contained herein is solely and universally available for information purposes. The data is presented without a warranty or promise of any kind.

The trademarks used are without approval, and the patent is issued without the trademark owner's permission or protection.

The logos and labels here are the possessions of the owners themselves and are not associated with this text.

CHAPTER 1: INTRODUCTION

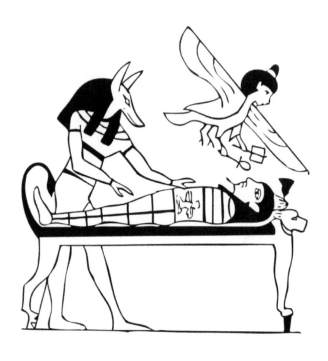

The crystal dates back to the era of history when the Earth was formed. The heating and cooling of the planet formed the impressive crystalline objects we have today. Gibbs gave the first prediction of crystal growth for natural mineral crystals. Many workers have contributed to the understanding of crystal growth. Curie and Wolf further developed the Gibbs surface theory. Former suggested that crystal growth occurs due to layer-by-layer adsorption of atoms or molecules on the crystal surface. It is termed as the theory of layer-by-layer growth. Later, other workers proposed some notable modifications to this theory. Well & Buckley gave an overview of the historical development of crystal growth theory. Physicists had a reasonable idea of how crystals would grow until 1940, but could not explain how crystals could simply initiate and build new layers with low levels of supersaturation. This issue leads to many amazing discoveries and unique depictions of crystals. Physicists again analyzed and calculated, but couldn't find a meaningful answer based on the old notion of crystal growth at the time. This issue was not resolved until British physicist F.C. Frank proposed a new modal in 1949. He pointed out that crystal growth could be explained simply, assuming that the layers are built up in a spiral by a continuous process rather than being placed on top of each other independently. It can occur if the crystal contains a type of defect known as a "screw dislocation."

In the case of a generalized model of crystal growth, in a series of four studies, the structural properties of the interface are negligible, not the binding energy between the molecules of the crystal and the liquid, such as full wetting or poor wetting. We had to wait until Temkin, who emphasized the frequent characterization. Crystal growth. It can be applied to any type of liquid crystal phase transformation. These are described in the literature in many theories of crystal growth, Chernoff & Muller Kulmvar, Marin, Goodman. From these different theories, it

14

can be concluded that the rate of crystal growth depends on the probability that an atom will find a place on the completed plane, not on the rate at which subsequent atoms are absorbed in the layer thus initiated. I will. Currently, a unified microscope interface theory of multi-component crystal growth is included. It also includes an approximation of the primary equation.

Crystal healing or crystal therapy is an increasingly popular method of energy healing. Although the healing of crystals may seem like a new era trend, crystals have been used therapeutically for thousands of years, and crystal talismans and amulets date back to the beginning of humanity. At a practical level, crystals have been used to improve our daily lives and scientific research. Crystals are used in watches, radios, lasers, and digital technology (to be precise, the device that read this). At the esoteric level, crystals have a long history in many cultures in Asia, Europe, and now, especially North America. From warriors to kings to local healers, crystals have been used for different purposes and different purposes. Amber Crystal is known for its practical and metaphysical ability to relieve physical pain and discomfort. Countless mothers have found a way to relieve baby pain, especially toothache, and make Baltic amber jewelry the most popular accessory for babies and children. Crystals are beautiful and fun, and their healing and energetic properties are available to everyone.

You do not need to be specially trained or subscribe to any particular belief system to use Crystal. All you need is to understand how they work, be open, ready to experiment, and profit for yourself. We are all composed of energy. Even everything is energy. Our body is dense energy that oscillates at a prolonged rate. So, we can see and feel them. But some other energetic beings and frequencies oscillate at a much faster rate than most of us cannot see with the naked eye. That does not mean they do not exist. We know this intuitively-every time someone advises to "read a room," they essentially intuitively grasp the energy in the room, whether they are positive or negative (High Frequency) and the appropriate procedure. When we are happy and peaceful, we emit high vibration frequencies that affect all the people around us. Being able to maintain this high level of vibration makes us feel like we are in front of us and makes everyone want to be together.

It works in both directions. If we are depressed or hostile, people can feel it too, and we negatively affect them. For example, I think most of us grew up just "knowing" before my parents said something when they were in a bad mood. We always influence people's energy. The energy frequency of crystals and gems is one of the highest vibration frequencies on earth. Our universe is based on the law of attraction. That is, it attracts other things whose vibrations match. In the presence of very high vibrations like a crystal, your energy state will begin to increase to match that of the crystal. It is essentially the way crystals affect us and the way crystal repair works. Each crystal has its energy properties. For example:

- Black Tourmaline has an astonishing grounding effect, which is especially useful for negative conversion and protection.
- Fluorite is especially useful for physical healing. Amethyst is also an effective healer and a perfect stone for anyone seeking spiritual healing and progress.

- Clear quartz must contain all the stone properties and can be universally used to enhance the effect of other stones.
- Rose Quartz is a famous "love stone" that, in addition to promoting and improving romantic love, is particularly useful for self-love, happiness, and peace care, as well as powerful healers and analgesics.
- As mentioned above, amber is an effective pain reliever and is most effective when touching the skin. Amber jewelry is available to children and adults in most baby boutiques, consignment stores, and online.

Using stones that suit your intention will improve and improve your results! Depending on what you need and the complexity you want to get things in, you can handle one stone or a variety of stones. Crystals can be put on the body, especially for pain relief, around you. The crystals can also be arranged in geometric patterns or crystal lattices, further enhancing the effect of the crystals. By the way, the use of crystals is not limited to physical and emotional healing, but you can use crystals to express things at the material level. Send happiness and love to yourself and your loved ones. It can also be sent as an encouragement to meditation. You can pull out the crystal during yoga practice to increase the energy in the room and enhance the positive effect of your practice. It can also be strategically placed throughout your living space to improve Feng Shui and add physical beauty and mood. There are so many ways to deal with crystals. The best way to deal with them is the one that works best for you then. The more complex ones are not always more effective. Consider flexibility for time constraints (such as deadlines) and resources (small collections may be sufficient). You don't have to follow the crystal lattice "recipe" strictly. Above all, let your intuition guide you. When working with energy, you need to be ready to leave your logical mind to an intuitive "heart." It is important to note that the term "cure" is used mainly in the context of general health and energy medicine. It does not mean "heal." Healing includes the well-being of body, mind, and soul. A sturdy person may be mentally disturbed, and usually ill patients have relatively maintained a high level of well-being (if he is in peace with his situation) and treat his pain/disorders to the extent of his ability).

Much of the "compression" of crystals and energy comes from what people interpret as a "miracle" cure for physical ailments, ranging from spontaneous bone formation to healthy recovery from illness. Furthermore, every crystal has properties that affect the body at a physical level that you can certainly use for your benefits. Importantly, crystal healing, like all energy healing modalities, acts on the body as a whole unit for the body, mind, and soul. Therefore, its effects are felt and experienced in a completely different way than traditional medicine. Because crystal energy affects the entire body, the crystal heals by restoring general health, including subtle bodies (invisible energetic bodies like the mental and emotional bodies). Traditional medicine is excellent as it divides the area being treated. The drug targets the virus/bacteria/disease in question and acts directly on its treatment. When medical intervention is required, Crystal is a great complementary therapy that can work synergistically with treatment to accelerate and improve the healing process. Crystals should not be used in place of drugs. Always consult with your doctor to get an appropriate diagnosis and determine what other treatments you may need.

If you're just starting with crystals, you can use their healing power by using Healing Stones to describe your intentions and what you want to make in your life. Apart from the crystals, these otherworldly rocks connect us to Earth because they are tangible physical forms with strong vibrations. This energy continues to connect with you as you bring these purposeful crystals closer to your skin and put them around you. By all thought and intent, these crystals absorb your unique vibrational energy and amplify the positive vibrations you have cultivated. In this magical world of vibrations, crystal energy keeps your intentions and reminds you of your connection to Earth, helping you on your spiritual journey. Such intentions are a starting point for healing the crystals, as the specific intentions that are built into common thinking patterns also become part of your energy. Clear quartz is always on earth, and ancient civilizations have used it as a protective talisman, peace offering, and gemstone. Quartz currently accounts for 12% of the Earth's crust and is used in almost every type of technology, including timekeeping, electronics, information storage, and more. If the crystal can communicate through the computer chip, isn't this vibrational energy transformed in another way? And it makes sense that crystals are universally healed by their connection to the Earth and its life-giving elements. Especially because it leaves a trail on us in almost every civilization. One of the first scientific proofs of the power of crystals is the work of IBM scientist Marcel Vogel. When I saw a crystal growing under a microscope, I noticed that it had all the shapes I imagined. He hypothesized that these vibrations are the result of the constant construction and destruction of intermolecular bonds. He also tested the spiritual power of the crystal and proved that the stone could store thoughts, as the band uses magnetic energy to absorb sound. Albert Einstein said that everything in life is vibration, and like sound waves, your thoughts match all the vibrations that appear in your life. So, if you believe that crystals have the potential for healing. The positive vibrations of the stone reinforce these thoughts. We always have the opportunity to choose our thoughts and present us with new challenges and great beginnings every day as we continue our journey. The healing crystals calm down the chat and remind us to reconnect with the earth's universal healing vibrations. An important lesson learned from crystals is patience. It is because working with the healing powers of crystals is just as time-consuming as these semi-precious stones were taking years to grow and deform. Learn, grow, and use crystals as you grow and remind yourself to appreciate the richness of Mother Nature and the great mysteries of the universe. Since healing crystals have been used for a long time, we have a wealth of knowledge and experience that has been passed down from generation to generation. If you know the basics of crystals, use your intuition to choose a healing stone for your spiritual journey. Crystal experts often say that Crystal chooses you and not the other way around. Walk around the room and see the crystals you notice. Whether attractive colors or other world shapes or patterns are fascinating, each crystal has its vibrational energy that removes blockages and prevents negative energy. Finding the right stone is the same in all wellness practices. It takes patience to calm and balance the body and mind. Hold the stone in your hand and calm down. Be careful if you feel any heat, cold, pulsation, calmness, etc. All these show that this particular stone is perfect for your healing needs. It also helps identify the specific problem or issue you are currently facing. If you have difficulty concentrating, fluorspar can help remove mental and emotional confusion and prevent concentration. Citrine makes your dreams come true by transmitting the positive vibrations of the sun to enrich your life. Carnelian is a powerful crystal that sheds creative juices. If you're struggling to let go of old ideas that are no longer useful, black tourmaline is a powerful gem that releases unwanted patterns that can be bad habits. It helps release all the negative energy in your body and your energy field. This stone also acts as a protective talisman. It is important if you are someone who easily absorbs the energy of others. Hematite is great for distracting other people by grounding you and reconnecting your mind to Earth's energy. If you are looking for more peace in your life, Amethyst is one of the crystals with the best intentions to relieve stress and rebalance your life. Another gem that balances emotions is the moonstone. It is useful when you are too emotional or untouched. Rose Quartz also opens and reconditions the heart chakra, which also helps with emotional well-being. It increases the feeling of self-love and unconditional love for others. Whether you're looking for gems for physical beauty or bringing peace to life, they all work to boost vibration frequencies. If you feel good, have a crystal in your hand, or are touching your skin, be prepared to have the opportunity to rock with this ancient healing art.

Thoughts create vibrations throughout the universe and are a powerful tool for achieving happiness and happiness. A specific purpose gives us an insight into our aspirations, dreams, and values. You can also live in the present moment without being caught in negative thought patterns. The intent is like a magnet. They attract what makes them happen. Setting goals is a powerful tool for achieving happiness. Creation a plan begins with setting goals that correspond to your values, aspirations, and goals.

- Decide what is important to you. Your values determine the behavior of your life, and if you want to find the satisfaction, you need to understand what is important to you for you.

- Explore areas of life that need upgrading. Think about how you can improve your relationship, your career, your social life, your spirituality, your health, and your community.

- Explain exactly what you need and why.

- Realize your intent. Certain rituals in the next chapter will ask you to write them down. Make sure you write them now as if they're happening, and check only what you want. You should also write down your goals, the result of what you want to reveal. With all your heart!

THE CHAKRAS

The human body is a container through which the spiritual energy known as Qi and Kundalini can flow. During the process of mental awakening, this energy passes through several energy centers throughout the body called chakras. The glandular system is the physical manifestation of the chakra. Chakras represented by colors within the spectrum of light frequencies and are associated with every aspect of life. The frequency of each color is important because it determines which chakra is related to the respective color. If the chakras are out of sync with other energy systems in the body, this process may transfer vibrational chain reactions to different chakras. It is essential to maintain a balanced chakra system, as chakras are as interdependent as life itself. The chakra system provides a framework for understanding humans in a way that

31

integrates the mind, body, and soul. "Chakra" is a Sanskrit word for wheel and is used to describe the vortex of energy in the field of human energy, first mentioned in Indian scriptures over 3,000 years ago. The chakra organizes the center for the absorption, assimilation, and transmission of life energy. Most Indian texts state that there are seven major chakras, each one at a specific point on the subtle body. They are associated with specific physical, psychological, and psychological problems.

Other spiritual traditions have 5, 8, 9, 12, or more chakras. The chakra is located along the spine and is often depicted as a lotus flower that opens upon spiritual development. Chakras can be active or dormant, depending on the state of consciousness. The Upanishad Chakra was first discovered in the Yoga Kundalini Upanishad (part of Krishnaya Jurveda) between 1400 and 1000 BC. The Upanishads were later between 200 BC. Written in 200 BC, the Shri Jabal Darshanaw Parishad, Kudama Niu Parishad, Yogatat Vau Parishad, Yoga Seekaupanishad, and Shandirau Parishad connected with chakras and subtle bodies.

Yoga Kudamani Upanishad said: The part made up of physical elements is called the "whole body" (sthula sharira). This subtle element is called the astral body (Sukushmasila). The part which includes all the causes that everyone has as an individual is called a causal body (Karanasharila). In the body of "(Honyama)" causality, three wildebeests (attributes), Satva (purity, wisdom, peace), Rajas (activity, passion), and Tamas (slow, lethargy) are entirely in harmony. However, in the astral and physical bodies, the balance between these gunas is lost, and dynamic interactions between them occur. Hiroshi Motoyama, Ph.D. Author" The theory of chakras: a bridge to a larger consciousness, "was discovered by modern science and technology because chakras are beyond the physical aspects. It was Dr. Motoyama said that this is not the center of energy. Chakras are the corresponding dimension and work. These features are closely related. Dr. Motoyama said, "The chakra is an exchange center between the body and the astral, and between the astral and the causal dimension."

Dr. Motoyama Says: "The chakras are also between the body and consciousness, between the astral body and the mana (heart), and between the causal relationships: it is an intermediary between all dimensions and other bodies and minds. The body and Karana (causal heart), along with the chakra, plays a role in the overall integration of the interrelationship among the three bodies and the mind. It has its sounds (Nada and Mantra) and geometric figures (Yantra) that can be perceived by the senses. The aura of the awakened chakra is brighter than the resting chakra. Even for the same person, the awakened chakras shine brighter than others. "Of course, a person's chakra is more active than others, but different people have different karmic and personal qualities. It is difficult to achieve enlightenment without awakening the chakra." An early version of the Nadi system is mentioned in Chandogya Upanishad, which is believed to be 3,000 years old. In this text, Nadis is compared to the rays of the sun. Yoga Shikka Upanishad states that the navel has its roots of 72,000 nadis. The word "Nad" means "movement" or "present."Nadis is a coarse and subtle body energy channel. Shiva Samhita says there are 350,000 Nadis in the body. Shiva Samhita is considered the most comprehensive dissertation on Hatha Yoga and is believed to have been written before 1500 BC. Written in BC There are two types of nadis, subtle and coarse. Gross Nadis-blood vessels, nerves, lymph vessels, veins. Subtle Nadis-The subtle energy channels are divided into two kinds: pranabahanadis and manovahanadis—Prana Baja Nadiscarries prana (life energy). The acupuncture meridian is the same as Prana Bahanadis.

ManovaHanadis wears "Manas Shakti" (mental energy). ManovaHanadis is a channel of mental energy and a channel of Chitta (impression) that results from feeling self. Prana is distributed to the body through thousands of channels. The Nadis system is connected to the spinal and peripheral nervous systems. Just as nerves send signals from the nervous system to glands, organs, and tissues, nadis distributes "prana" into the body and transforms it into various forms of life energy suitable for multiple organs, glands, and tissues.

There are 14 major nadis. The three big nadis are Sushumna, Idā, and Pingala. Sushumna Nadi is the central integrated channel that connects the chakras and their different levels of consciousness. Idenandi and Pingaranandi are two channels on either side of the spine. Pingaranandi is linked to solar energy. The word Pingala has many meanings in Sanskrit. It means "fire," "snake," "reddish-brown, tan, yellow, golden."Pingaranandi has a sunlike character and masculine energy. The temperature warms and moves from the man's right testicle to his right nostril. In women, Pingalanadi starts from the right side of the primary chakra. IdāNadi is associated with the energy of the moon. The word Idu means "comfort" in Sanskrit. Nato Ito has a moonlike nature and feminine energy and has a cooling effect. Move from male left testicle to left nostril. For women, Idonandi begins on the left side of the base chakra. Dr.Motoyama says 14 major nadis closely match the acupuncture meridians of Chinese medicine. He said SushumnaNadi corresponds to the Governor of the (Du Mai) Governor Ship Meridian in Chinese medicine. However, you can also connect to a penetrating vessel (Chennai). He says that Idunandi and Pingaranandi are connected to the outer bladder meridians that flow to both sides of the spine.

SEVEN CHAKRAS - ASSOCIATIONS

1. Chakrawan (Earth element) -Base of the spine-Coccygeal Plexus-Survival-Urogenital System-Adrenal gland

2. Chakra 2 (water element) -lower abdomen-plexus sacral-reproductive and genitourinary system-gonads
3. Chakra 3 (element of fire) -abdomen-solar plexus-personal power, digestion, metabolic energy-pancreas
4. Chakra Four (Air Elements) -Sternum-Cardiac Plexus-Love-Thymus
5. Chakra Five (acoustic element) -neck area-pharyngeal plexus-creativity, communication-thyroid
6. Chaclassics (Light Element) -Center of Forehead-Intuition, Imagination, Perspective-Pituitary
7. Chakra assists in Seven-Crown-Enlightenment, Knowledge, Understanding-Controlling every aspect of the body. Along with that mind-Imbalances and limitations of energy flow within the pineal, chakra is unresolved emotions, traumas,

thought patterns that are caused by past actions, restrictive beliefs, and the negative ones. Chakra balance can be restored by yoga, meditation, tai chi, breathing, massage, energy medicine, and healing.

Chakra Colors compiled in 1577, and each chakra is said to have some petals, colors, and Villa Mantras. (Arthur Avalon, The Power of the Snake 1974).

1. Chakra One (Muradara) -4 Petals-Yellow-LAM
2. Chakra Two (Svadisthana) -6 Petals-White-VAM
3. Chakraslee (Manipura) -10 petals-red-RAM
4. Chakra Four-12 Petals-Gray-YAM
5. Chakra Five (Vishudda) -16 Petals-White-HAM

6. Cha Classics (Ajuna) -2 or 96 petals-White / Silver-OM

7. Chakra Seven (Sahasrara) -1,000 petals-Gold-silence or all sounds.

The leading authority on the chakra, Harish Johari, is similar in color to the chakra in his book "Energy Center of Transformation."

1. Madara-yellow, red petals

2. Svadisthana-transparent with white / light blue / red petals

3. Manila-Red and Blue Petals Anahata-Colorless / Smoky Gray / Smoky Green and Red Petals

4. Vishuddha-Smoky purple with lavender gray and purple petals

5. Arjuna-White / Luminous / Bluish / Camphor white and light blue petals

6. Sahasrara-all colors with iridescent petals.

In 1977 Christopher Hills published a book called "Nuclear Evolution." He was the first person to combine chakra and rainbow colors. In Upanishad, there is no relationship between chakras and rainbow colors. Kundalini is the energy ("Shakti") that must wrap around the base of the spine. Kundalini is seen as a goddess waiting to wake up or a sleeping snake. Awakening in Kundalini is said to lead to deep meditation, enlightenment, and bliss. This awakening involves Kundalini Shakti moving each chakra to Shmunana Andy to reach the crown chakra. Many yoga systems focus on kundalini awakening through meditation, pranayama (breathing), asana (posture), and singing mantras. Many describe Kundalini's movement as a current flowing through the spine. When Kundalini's energy penetrates all chakras, it brings a spiritual awakening to a person. Once the Kundalini journey is complete, you should be fully enlightened.

In addition to the Kundalini flowing from the root chakra to the crown chakra, energy flows from the crown chakra to the base chakra. This energy flows out of the spiritual realm and allows us to reveal our unique purpose in our lives. Together, the two energy streams form an energy balance between the body (material) and the mind (consciousness). With these free streams of energy, we can live now and beyond. (Judith Anodea, Wheels of Life, 1990) A chakra is a connection point where energy flows from one body to another. Seers can see Ether's second chakra. They appear as saucer-like depressions on the surface of the vortex.

When they are undeveloped, they look like small circles about 5 cm in diameter and glow weakly in the average person. But when it wakes up, it becomes enormous and looks

43

like vertebrae burning like the sun. "We sometimes say that they correspond loosely to certain body organs. They appear on a well-ventilated double surface, slightly protruding from the dense contours of the body. Directly on bindweed bells, take a look and imagine the general look of the chakras: each flower stem comes from the point of the spine, in different views. Also, the spine can be manifested as the central stem, from which the flowers are spaced to the branch and show the opening of the bell on the surface of the ether body. Life from the back of the sun logo (the ray of love), this is called the main force. But one is usually better than the other: "Without this energy surge, the body couldn't exist. So, the center is run by everyone, but usually in power. Only required vertebrae It is a relatively slow movement of the undeveloped people to form. In more developed humans, they can shine and pulsate in living light, and a large amount of energy flows through them, thus adding additional abilities and possibilities. Gender is available to humans." Chakras can divide into three groups.

1. Physically
2. Personally, base and spleen
3. Solar plexus, heart, neck mental
4. The third eye, the crown chakra, exists in both the ether and astral dimensions.

He states that the astral chakras are only active when Kundalini is active alone. Both astral and etheric chakras must be awakened so that one can be aware of the astral dimension. The astral chakra is like the sensory organ of the astral body. As soon as the first astral chakras become active, Kundalini will raise them and activate each one in turn.

1. First Chakra-Home of the Snake Fire
2. Second Chakra-Enables in-vitro experience
3. Third Chakra-Enables sensitivity to astral energy
4. Force Chakra-You can feel the feeling of being Astral
5. Fifth Chakra-You can hear the existence of Astral
6. Six Chakras-Enable Astral Vision
7. Seventh Chakra-Enables full recognition of the astral world

How can I tell if the chakra is blocked? So how do you know if the chakras are blocked? That's a good question. The following are some of the signs and symptoms that can result from one or more blocked chakras.

1. Hard to sleep
2. Difficult to concentrate
3. Chronic depression or anxiety

4. Mood swings

5. Communication problems

6. Difficult to connect with others

7. I feel stuck

Which chakra is blocked? If you give your chakra a little TLC, then all that one thing is to know: the chakras that are blocked. If you want to use the knowledge to open chakras, you need to know which chakras you need to process. So how do you identify on which chakra you should work? If you feel that something in your life is out of balance, this imbalance is usually energy in one of your chakras. It can be attributed to the interruption. Are you struggling to speak for yourself? The throat chakra may be blocked. Are you suffering from chronic anxiety? The root chakra may be out of hand. Deborah King, the author of Mindvalley's Be A Modern Master Program, explains: "All spiritual progress comes from self-confidence." Take a step back and look into your life. Where are the shortages and imbalances? Listen to your instincts and identify the chakras that need to be opened.

4 WAYS TO OPEN A CHAKRA TO INCREASE YOUR HEALTH IF YOU WANT TO LEARN HOW TO OPEN A CHAKRA YOURSELF, THERE ARE SEVERAL WAYS:

1. CHAKRA MEDITATION

This is probably one of the most influential and reliable ways to open a chakra. Chakra meditation, however, requires a more aggressive approach than most others. This is a high starting point when you're ready to get the problem into your hands. Guided chakra meditation guides you through the steps of focusing your energy where your body needs most. It's best to practice this a few times to make it last, but it's worth it in the long run.

2. STRENGTHEN MUDRA

Mudra is a unique hand position that can activate and open the chakra. Each chakra has its corresponding mudra. You can practice Mudra yourself, but Mudra is best practiced with Chakra Meditation.

3. CLEAN MANTRA

Another way to increase the effectiveness of chakra meditation is to add some mantras. A sound is assigned to each chakra. Singing the chakra sound activates the stagnant energy that blocks the chakra you want to open.

4. CHAKRA JEWELRY

When we interact with crystals, their energy frequencies affect ours. Individual crystals can also affect our physical and mental health. Each chakra is responsible for various physiological and psychological functions. Carrying single glasses or storing them in a nearby house can facilitate the transfer of energy through specifically blocked chakras.

CHAKRA HEALING CRYSTALS AND STONES

Crystals have existed on Earth for thousands of years and are unique in having a perfect atomic structure/energy balance. These structures allow them to function as transmitters, reservoirs, and reflectors of cosmic energy contained deep inside the earth. They have particular properties that enable them to receive, focus, and transform energy. Crystals are used to amplify radio sound waves and television light waves. Crystals can be passive or active. For example, crystals are widely used in healing and meditation practices to focus and redirect energy in many positive ways. Crystals can restore the energy balance of a room by leaving it in your place or workplace. You can wear a crystal around your neck, in your pocket, or during meditation. Our thoughts, feelings, and desires are also energy, so we can use crystals to improve our meditation and confirmation exercises.

CHOOSING CRYSTALS

Finding the crystals that you attract is essential. There is no definite rule of what does not makes a proper crystal. More significant, more expensive crystals don't necessarily mean better for you. Finding the perfect crystal for you is a journey of energy.

It is advisable to choose your crystals from the heart because what you are trying to reveal is the desire of your heart. A simple exercise is to hold it in your hand for a few minutes, take your consciousness into your breath, and stay there. You may soon be attracted to the crystal. I can ask a question in my head. You will know again whether it is the right crystal for you. All crystals are focused on different strengths and areas you can focus on. Includes seven significant chakras to support healing, cleansing, meditation, and confirmation exercises.

CRYSTALS AND THE CHAKRAS

Each chakra also has tuned chakra-colored healing crystals and gems that can be used to repair the crystals. Healing chakra colors can have significant physical, emotional, and emotional effects. When our chakras are blocked or drained, our bodies, minds, and souls are unable to function correctly. Clarifying and balancing chakras with chakra color, crystals, chakra sounds, breaths, and positive confirmations can quickly and effectively return to a vibrant and healthy balance.

SOME MAJOR CHAKRAS, THEIR COLORS, AND STONES ROOT

Red Black Brown Gray Garnet, Onyx, Jasper, Ruby, Bloodstone Sakura Orange Carnelian, Moonstone, Tourmaline, Yellow Jasper, Sonnenstein Solar Plexus Yellow Citrine, Yellow Sapphire, Calcite Orange, Ametrine, Hematite, Amber, Tiger Eye, Citrine, Gold Topaz, Agate Heart Green Pink Rose Quartz, Green Tourmaline, Kunzite, Emerald, Green Jade, Quartz, Amazonite, Chrysocolla, Rhodonite, Aventurine Neck Chakra Sky Blue, Aqua, Turquoise Turquoise, Blue Menow, Chalcedony, Aquamarine, Black

Onyx, Mauri Greenstone, Quartz Amount / Third Door Indigo, purple, dark blue sodalite, lapis lazuli, opal, sodalite, fluorite, lepidolite, quartz crown violet, white, gold amethyst, clear quartz, topaz, sapphire, garnet, smoky quartz.

CHAKRA CRYSTAL MEDITATION PREPARATION

Crystal meditation is the use of crystals to achieve specific results during meditation. You can use any stone, but quartz is a master crystal, which is especially useful, but you can use it. When handling crystals to help meditation, you may be able to inspire various gifts and talents. It depends on what you want to do as a result. There are several different outcomes we want to achieve with this practice. Select one or more stones for each previously washed chakra. Even if you have the chakras you need, you may want to balance all the chakras. When lying down, place each stone in the proper place on the bed or next to the chakra. I would like to have a clear quartz point with one hand, and a rose quartz with the other side. When sitting, you can hold the crystal in your hand, place it under a chair, or combine both.

AS YOUR AWARENESS INCREASES

After practicing this for a while, you may want to visualize the colors associated with each chakra as the breath passes through the relevant parts of the body. If you are working on a particular chakra, you can issue a confirmation. For example, the evidence for the fourth chakra would be: "Give unconditional love." Repeat the proof yourself. Imagine that you are full of colored roses. Introduce yourself to a loved situation. You cannot overbalance your chakras. It is an easy way to relax. As you continue to practice it, you will feel more focused on your subtle energy. They notice an imbalance before physically expressing themselves.

Crystals have been a part of human history since the beginning. It is not only the appearance of these dazzling stones but their overwhelming energy that has attracted civilization. From supernatural properties to extraterrestrial properties, crystals provide many incredible powers, such as healing heart disease anxiety. Combine that with incense, and you'll have the perfect therapy for your home! Scientifically speaking, the unique arrangement of atoms in a crystal and its crystallization process determines the forces it contains. Due to changes in color, origin, and variety, each crystal exhibits a different and unique effect. Crystal Chakra Activation for Chakra Power Known as the seven power or energy points of the body, is one of the crystal's most magnificent magical properties. Translated as a ring of light from Sanskrit, the imbalanced chakras lead to physical, metaphysical, and emotional disabilities. The electromagnetic fields emitted by your body when resonating with aura, or bright colors, produce positive vibrations and results.

FIVE HEALING CRYSTALS THAT ACTIVATE CHAKRA POWER ARE ELABORATED HERE:

I. TIGER'S EYE

1. ORIGIN

Tiger Eye Crystal is a distance crystal from India, Burma, Brazil, South Africa, Western Australia, and the United States.

2. COLOR ENERGY

The Tiger Eye represents a bright ray of gold that brings success and happiness.

3. TYPES OF TIGER EYE

Tiger Eye Crystal, Blue Gray, Red Tiger Eye, Tiger Eye Matrix.

4. CHAKRA POWER

Wearing a Tiger Eye carries not only the Kundalini energy but also the chakras such as the roots, sacrum, and solar plexus.

5. SPIRITUAL BENEFIT

The crystal of a tiger's eye, the crystal of a psychic gift, resonates with the frequency of the earth. The tiger's eye crystal is a spiritually nourishing stone that promotes promotion. Wearing a Tiger Eye Crystal will keep your yin and yang motivated and balanced. It also extends lively ideas as well as intuitive power.

6. PHYSICAL USE

Tiger eye crystals target the endocrine system and balance both hemispheres in the brain. Tiger Eye Crystal also cures asthma, bone disease, high blood pressure, bladder, and digestive problems.

7. EMOTIONAL INFLUENCE

Tiger's eye crystals promote emotional well-being, relieve depression, and permanently stop nightmares. Tiger's eyes release hidden fear and stabilize emotional turbulence. Longwear also enhances user patience, passion, honesty, and optimism.

8. AFFORDABLE SOLUTION

Grab this macho bracelet with tiger eye crystals and flexible rubber bands. Fabulous jewelry fits your goals!

PERIDOT

Origin Peridot is sourced from countries such as Pakistan, Australia, Ireland, Russia, Sri Lanka, USA, Egypt, and Brazil.

TYPES OF PERIDOT

1. CHAKRA POWER

The stone of fate is ideal for activating the chakras of the heart and solar plexus.

2. SPIRITUAL BENEFIT

In addition to a positive power, Peridot reveals fate silences religious fears and helps ease karmic debt. Known as the Elven Stone, Peridot was also the horoscope for St. Bartholomew's and was best suited for healing animals and the Earth. Crystal healers have proposed to shine golden stars through Peridot on sunny afternoons to cure asthma and other respiratory disorders. Wearing peridot balances the endocrine system and concentrates on the adrenal glands, digestive tract, gallbladder, liver, spleen, and pancreas. Peridot also heals astigmatism, myopia, and tired eyes, ensuring a healthy pregnancy.

3. EMOTIONAL INFLUENCE

Peridot is recommended to relieve the tension known as the butterfly. It cures many mental disorders, such as bipolar disorder, depression, and depression. You can also use it for emotional pain like tattered ego, anger, jealousy, rebellion, and resentment, or just for satisfaction.

4. COLOR ENERGY

Peridot is a crystal that fulfills its purpose and represents the energy of the colors green (growth) and yellow (sunlight).

5. AFFORDABLE SOLUTION

Try these charming 18ct gold-plated peridot studs in a beautiful setting and instantly recall past life and peace!

II. MOONSTONE

1. ORIGIN

Famous travel stones come from India, China, Brazil, Madagascar, North America, Tanzania, Europe, and Sri Lanka.

2. COLOR ENERGY

Moonstone, the stone of Goddess Diana, expresses her values as white color and purity, innocence, and unity.

3. TYPES OF MOONSTONE

Cat Eye Moonstone (or Blue), Gray, White, Peach, Yellow, Rainbow Moonstone.

4. CHAKRA POWER

Known to increase Kundalini energy in men and women. Placing Moonstone in the crown or solar plexus chakra will activate the chakra power.

5. SPIRITUAL BENEFIT

Moonstone is known as a sacred stone or crystal of God and Goddess. Mentally eliminates the denial of ego and material interests. Moonstone is considered ideal for hermits and priests, helping to open their minds and improve their synchronicity, chances, and perceptions.

6. PHYSICAL USE

It is used for resetting the ideal of the body clock. Wearing Moonstone increases fertility and reduces menstrual problems, insomnia, sleepwalking, sleep deprivation, hair, skin, eye, and organ damage. Moonstone helps promote detoxification in addition to healing digestive and excretory disorders.

7. EMOTIONAL INFLUENCE

Moonstone is an ideal crystal to help you master your emotions. It helps stabilize emotional health and promotes confidence and thinking. Moonstone is a comfortable crystal known for stopping nightmares. It also helps heal emotional trauma, stress, and anxiety.

8. AFFORDABLE SOLUTION

This cute Cat Eye Moonstone Apple Charm sheds sweet energy and is a great reason to buy and wear it to unleash your hidden potential.

III.   LABRADORITE

1. ORIGIN

The Inuit says that Labradorite was born in Aurora Borealis but came from Madagascar, Mexico, Russia, Italy, Norway, Finland, India, America, Newfoundland, and Australia.

2. COLOR ENERGY

Labradorite represents an element of ice, a blue color, which promotes trust and responsibility.

3. CHAKRA POWER

The Magic Crystal is a combination of most chakras but works best when held over chakra points such as the neck, solar plexus, or crown.

4. SPIRITUAL BENEFIT

Labradorite, known for its increased synchronicity and serendipity, improves aura, positivity, communication skills, psychological talent, and mental energy through hallucinations. Labradorite also prevents energy loss and is ideal for artists.

5. PHYSICAL USE

Labradorite users will benefit from increased metabolism and weight loss. It helps treat lungs, respiratory tract, gastrointestinal tract, blood pressure, cold, rheumatism, menstrual cramps, gout, eye diseases.

6. EMOTIONAL INFLUENCE

Labradorite relieves anxiety, brightens the mood, and promotes user creativity, making it ideal for restless people. Labradorite also helps relief from passion, rejuvenation, reflection, determination, illusion, peace, and anxiety, and to strengthen trust in nature.

7. AFFORDABLE SOLUTION

Open your crown chakra with four packs of this 100% mighty labradorite cane to heal and discover your potential!

IV.   LAPIS LAZULI

1. ORIGIN

Heavenly Blue Crystal is manufactured in countries such as Egypt, Chile, Italy, Russia, and the United States.

2. COLOR ENERGY

Lapis lazuli emits a deep blue color that represents robust and compassionate energy.

3. CHAKRA POWER

Lapis Lazuli is the commanding crystal and activates the crown and neck chakras.

4. SPIRITUAL BENEFIT

Lapis lazuli not only opens the third eye but also guarantees active peace of mind. Lapis lazuli promises peace by naturally releasing your energy from the lower chakra to the upper chakra. Lapis lazuli means progress, bringing clarity, higher consciousness, and spiritual gifts such as your connection with your guardian angel.

5. PHYSICAL USE

By wearing lapis lazuli on the neck, larynx, vocal cords, thyroid, ears, and nose can help alleviate many illnesses. Some notable physical disorders that are cured by crystals are sleep deprivation, dizziness, high blood pressure, skin conditions, allergies, inflammation, autism, Asperger's syndrome, encephalopathy, and migraine.

6. EMOTIONAL INFLUENCE

Lapis lazuli activates the feelings of empathy, honor, and grace, and shows suppressed emotions. Also, wearing crystals at all times can enhance your self-confidence and eliminate self-pity, depression, and inferiority.

7. AFFORDABLE SOLUTION

The 3.5-ounce natural lapis lazuli crystal stone best-selling pack is available in its natural form. Installing it in your office or home maximizes your emotional freedom.

IN A NUTSHELL

Placing and placing crystals on top of each chakra helps create each positive vibration that brings health, prosperity, and spiritual community. Get the full set of POWERFUL 7 Chakra Generators with 7 points to rejuvenate your chakra power and recognize hidden potentials!

The best way to get rid of chakra problems is to wear a pendant made from a complete set of chakra crystals, such as B. Eagle or Yogi shaped mixed stone chakra pendant!

CHAPTER 2: DISCOVERING CRYSTALS' HIDDEN POWER

The logic of the work behind using crystals to cure physical ailments is energy. With the help of crystal energy, you can even detoxify your body and soothe your intolerable pain. If you need urgent medical advice, you should replace the crystal with medicine as soon as possible. However, when using crystals in addition to pharmaceuticals, the results are doubly effective.

Crystals on the body can be helpful in digestive, reproductive, excretory, circulatory, and respiratory disorders.

FIVE CRYSTALS THAT CURES PHYSICAL ILLNESSES

V. AMETHYST

1. ORIGIN

Amethyst is known as the Crystal or Royal Family and occurs only in Namibia and South Africa.

2. COLOR ENERGY

Amethyst is a precious gem and combines red and purple colors.

3. AMETHYST TYPE

Brandberg amethyst, chevron amethyst, taconite, ametrine, amethyst rutile can be enlisted here.

4. CHAKRA POWER

Amethyst represents the sweet energy of the chakra-the, the third eye, and the crown.

5. SPIRITUAL BENEFIT

Wearing amethyst in major chakras also opens psychological and spiritual channels through the body. Amethyst has astral predictions of intellectual contact with shamanic motives and rational thinking and has many religious uses.

6. PHYSICAL USE

The psychologically protective crystals are also optimal for immunity, strengthening the sympathetic nervous system and endocrine glands. Always wear amethyst. It will reduce bruising, gastrointestinal disorders, stomach, skin, and heart problems.

7. EMOTIONAL INFLUENCE

Amethyst is a staunch defender of cognitive perception. Creativity, passion, and fantastic stress management empower users. Amethyst is not only comfortable in despair but also ideal for any challenge.

8. AFFORDABLE SOLUTION

Buy this gorgeous purple with white stripes and 100g of Amethyst Crystal Wand and get rid of your worst fear and flu forever!

VI.   TOPAZ

1. ORIGIN

Stones of Light or Topaz come from countries such as Brazil, Nigeria, Burma, Australia, Mexico, and Germany.

2. COLOR ENERGY

Colorless crystals are another unique stone that is unaffected by light.

3. TOPAZ TYPES

Blue topaz, white or silver topaz, pink topaz, a purple topaz, imperial topaz, brown topaz, mysterious topaz, rutile topaz is some of the type.

4. CHAKRA POWER

Topaz is one of the most different crystals on the market, activating the neck, solar plexus, and sacral chakra.

5. SPIRITUAL BENEFIT

They are known for reducing mental weight, and by wearing topaz, the meditative crystal produces peace and reintegration into universal power in addition to Christ's consciousness. They also help to recognize higher areas of knowledge, divinity, wisdom, serenity, and spiritual connection.

6. PHYSICAL USE

Topaz is 100% by stabilizing hypertension and reducing headache, migraine, jaw elevation, occipital headache, sore throat, language problems, colds, influenza, pneumonia, allergies, asthma, and autism. It makes them healthier.

7. EMOTIONAL INFLUENCE

Topaz is the ideal crystal for polishing your intelligence and resolving fear, uncertainty, or doubt. It also strengthens your trust. Wearing topaz eliminates psychological problems such as stress, schizophrenia, spinal disorders, and identity disorders.

8. AFFORDABLE SOLUTION

Connect with the karma of your previous life with this meditative crystal with the power of fortune-telling energy with this stunning 12-in-1 Rainbow Mystic Topaz pendant.

VII.   GARNET

1. ORIGIN

Garnet is known as a health stone and comes from countries such as Mozambique, Africa, Brazil, Sri Lanka, USA, India, Madagascar, and Canada.

2. COLOR ENERGY

Garnets are protective crystals that respond to most colors, but most are grounded in scarlet or red.

3. GARNET SEEDS

Pyrope garnet, Radit garnet, Uvarovite garnet, Grossler garnet.

4. CHAKRA POWER

Garnet promotes Kundalini energy and is ideal for wearing on the solar plexus, heart, or crown chakra.

5. SPIRITUAL BENEFIT

Garnets are known for increasing productivity, converting negative energy into positive energy, and helping to sharpen your perception. Garnets are mysterious crystals that help expand your knowledge and prevent evil vibrations. It is also a stone of wisdom.

6. PHYSICAL USE

In the past, garnets were amulets for travelers and were known for promoting libido, splenic disorders, arthritis, rheumatism, fatigue, and alleviating blood clots. Wearing garnet not only stabilizes your deficiency of iodine, magnesium, vitamins A and D but also helps you lose weight and cleanse your DNA.

7. EMOTIONAL INFLUENCE

Garnet is known to increase self-confidence and cure mental disorders such as clinical depression. Placing the garnet under the pillow also eases terrible dreams, fears, and despair. Wear garnets to promote survival instinct, uplifting posture, or self-esteem.

8. AFFORDABLE SOLUTION

Check out this gold-plated authentic garnet ring made of 925 sterling silver. Citrine is seductively set to enhance the health pink and the health of loved ones.

VIII.   ONYX

1. ORIGIN

Onyx is a drinking stone from Brazil, Afghanistan, India, Uruguay, Madagascar, Mexico, Peru, and the United States.

2. COLOR ENERGY

Onyx is a black power crystal that represents purity and purity.

3. TYPES OF ONYX

Black onyx, white onyx, and onyx pebbles are the types.

4. CHAKRA POWER

Crystal healers argued that onyx works in all chakras, but especially in the heart, root, and solar plexus chakras.

5. SPIRITUAL BENEFIT

Wearing onyx, known as the stone of reason and patience, helps to focus and rejuvenate the energy field. Onyx can also help calm and radiate positive thinking for those who tend to get angry quickly. In addition to the shield from the negative, it is a crystal that cultivates intuitive power.

6. PHYSICAL USE

Onyx is a powerful crystal in the removal of poisoning and helps relieve blood, teeth, bones, eyes, bone marrow, feet, kidneys, and heart disease. Wearing onyx is also great for treating epilepsy and glaucoma.

7. EMOTIONAL INFLUENCE

Onyx reflects protection stones that protect users in addition to their confidence and strength. Teaching self-control, reasoning, and self-control alleviate stress, anxiety, and depression.

8. AFFORDABLE SOLUTION

This fabulous onyx black pendant is a black pendant made of 925 sterling silver, perfect for protection from disease and curses.

IX.   SAPPHIRE

1. ORIGIN

Sapphire is one of the four most precious stones in the world and comes from Sri Lanka, Australia, Madagascar, India, Thailand, Brazil, and Burma.

2. COLOR ENERGY

The energy of sky colors like blue and indigo indicate that sapphire emphasizes elements of trust and honor.

3. SAPPHIRE TYPE

Black sapphire, orange sapphire, violet sapphire, yellow sapphire, green sapphire, white sapphire, star sapphire, and pink sapphire are to be considered here.

4. CHAKRA POWER

A robust blue wisdom stone made of sapphire crystal activates the neck and third eye chakra.

5. SPIRITUAL BENEFIT

Sapphire conveys prophetic enlightenment and is the epitome of prosperity. Within a day, sapphire works with users to develop intuitive skills to improve learning ability, trans sensor perception, and memory of past lives.

6. PHYSICAL USE

Known for relieving fever, throat problems, digestion, tuberculosis, fatigue, heart disease, eye infections, and insomnia, wearing sapphire relieves burns and activates endocrine glands. Sapphire is a purification stone that can also help with dizziness, dementia, and blood disorders.

7. EMOTIONAL INFLUENCE

Wind stone is an ideal crystal for practicing self-discipline, honesty, concentration, mental clarity, and serenity. Sapphire not only makes dreams come true, but it also alleviates depression, inferiority, and mood swings.

8. AFFORDABLE SOLUTION

With a 55% discount, this stunning Blue Sapphire Stone Ring is an excellent accessory that blends into most personalities and heals your heart!

IN A NUTSHELL

The effect of using a crystal for physical healing depends on where and how the crystal is used. Rub the crystal on the painful or uncomfortable area. Another way is to meditate with them. You can also place the crystals as bracelets or necklaces in specific areas of the bedroom.

This Amethyst Garnet Topaz 925 Silver Ring comes with a unique healing crystal for your body's energy to heal many ailments of your body.

CHAPTER 3: HIDDEN POWER AND HEALING STONES

Did you know that crystals are an essential part of the effective love spell of centuries ago?

Crystals like Rose Quartz help find true love, from regaining the urge from self-love to love. Love crystals are combined with vibrations that activate and radiate love vibrations. These stones resonate with Anahata or the heart chakra.

These crystals are also ideal for promoting love. They now combine the right frequencies based on the energy of color to attract your true love!

5 CRYSTALS THAT ATTRACT LOVE AND COMPASSION

1. ROSE QUARTZ

1. ORIGIN

Rose Quartz stands for Great Mother and comes from Japan, India, South Africa, South Dakota, Brazil, and Madagascar.

2. COLOR ENERGY

Rose quartz oscillates gently and exhibits a pleasing color of energy such as bright reds and pinks.

3. TYPE

Crystalline rose quartz and pink quartz.

4. CHAKRA POWER

Balancing the energy of yin and yang and opening the heart by activating the heart chakra is a vital force of rose quartz.

5. SPIRITUAL BENEFIT

Rose quartz is a delicate crystal that heals from the inside and helps connect with the vibrations of the universe. The release of waves of love and the wearing of rose quartz help heal old wounds and love them again.

6. PHYSICAL USE

Wearing Rose Quartz on your sternum will relieve burns and blisters, leaving you with clear skin free from free radicals and wrinkles. In addition to dizziness, decreased libido, and infertility rose quartz also cures cardiovascular, heart, and respiratory tract illnesses.

7. EMOTIONAL INFLUENCE

Rose quartz is excellent for letting go of old love and developing sensuality. It eliminates suffering, fear, expectations, and depression. It also promotes fulfillment, peace of mind, joy, positive self-image, compassion, and self-esteem.

8. **AFFORDABLE SOLUTION**

Alti Lady Rose Quartz is noble rose quartz hung on a gold chain. It's an ideal necklace to amplify your love vibrations!

2. OPAL

1. ORIGIN

Popular ice tones come from America, Brazil, Peru, Mexico, and Australia.

2. COLOR ENERGY

As one of the unique crystals with the full color of the rainbow, opal drives all the colors.

3. OPAL TYPES

Fire Opal, Rainbow Opal, Pochopal, Andes Opal, Black Opal, Boulder Opal, Crystal Opal Phrase Opal, Matrix Opal, Milk Opal, Moss Opal, Water Opal, Wood Opal.

4. CHAKRA POWER

Wearing opal activates most chakras, including the heart, crown, neck, sacrum, and roots.

5. SPIRITUAL BENEFIT

Opal has always been a crystal used by humans and is known for its imagination and creativity. Opal is composed primarily of water and is an ideal Waterstone for carrying and treating change. It helps you transform and obscure you whenever you want, in addition to astral projection and spiritual power.

6. PHYSICAL USE

Opal is a protective stone known to relieve headaches, insulin regulation, sexual disorders, menstrual pain, bone disorders, dizziness, neuropathy, loss of appetite, and fatigue. Also ideal for Parkinson's disease.

7. EMOTIONAL INFLUENCE

Opal is a crystal whose loyalty is rooted in relationships. It brings emotional freedom, happiness, self-confidence, and the reproduction of buried emotions such as passion and love. Wearing opal promotes not only personal strength but also peace and happiness.

8. AFFORDABLE SOLUTION

This stunning Australian Opal ring with white fire is not only aesthetically pleasing but also has the breathtaking power of crystal for its purity, innocence, and charm.

3. AGATE

1. ORIGIN

Agate Lucky Crystals are from the Middle East, South Africa, Egypt, and Russia.

2. COLOR ENERGY

Agate has a pure color tone and is a crystal of courage.

3. TYPES OF AGATE

Blue Race Agate, Turritella Agate, Crazy Race Agate, Dendrite Agate, Moss Agate, Laguna Agate, Fire Agate.

4. CHAKRA POWER

Agate is known for balancing yin and yang. It is useful when placed in the solar plexus.

5. SPIRITUAL BENEFIT

In contrast to most healing crystals, agate oscillates at slow frequencies, promoting collective consciousness, reintegration into the universe, and internal stability. Agate also releases negative energy, helping a focus of relaxation and meditation.

6. PHYSICAL USE

When worn during labor, agate reduces the appearance of baby blue, and when worn by the mother on the sternum promotes breastfeeding. The best physical healing properties of agate are the stomach, uterus, intestines, eyes, skin, immunity, myocardium, gums, teeth, and circadian rhythm.

7. EMOTIONAL INFLUENCE

Agate crystals are ideal for promoting tranquility, self-confidence, and practical thinking. It teaches us to extend our perception and accept love. Agate also relieves stress, nightmares, and anxiety.

8. AFFORDABLE SOLUTION

Amazing to see, these irregularly shaped natural agate stone pendants are spiritually and physically sublime. Wear it or keep it at home and develop your love for a new life.

4. BLOODSTONE

1. ORIGIN

Known as the Stone of Courage, Bloodstone comes from India, China, the United States, Australia, Brazil, and the Kathiawar Peninsula.

2. COLOR ENERGY

Bloodstone stands for green or the energy of growth.

3. CHAKRA POWER

Bloodstone, which resonates with vitality, activates the chakra power of the sacrum, roots, and heart.

4. SPIRITUAL BENEFIT

Wearing Bloodstone is ideal for increasing mental tolerance, confusion, and positive solutions. It promotes a feeling of peace and strength. Known as the Martyr's Stone, Bloodstone also helps rebalance the spirit.

5. PHYSICAL USE

Bloodstone users are not affected by gastric, intestinal, bladder, or blood illnesses. Wearing Bloodstone during pregnancy also guarantees painless delivery. It is also effective against hemorrhoids, insect bites, menopausal pain, and hormonal imbalance.

6. EMOTIONAL INFLUENCE

Bloodstone promotes courage, determination, transformation, and emotional stability. Martyr's Stone helps to recognize the goals of life, shed the fear of death, promote truth and love, and self-sufficiency.

7. AFFORDABLE SOLUTION

Place Bloodstone under the pillow while you sleep.

5. JADE
1. ORIGIN

Jade is called the Stone of Life and comes from Burma, USA, Russia, Zimbabwe, Cuba, Turkey, Poland, Australia, Japan, Canada, Taiwan, and China.

2. COLOR ENERGY

Jade represents the vitality of creation or green.

3. JADE TYPE

White jade, Indian jade, lavender jade, black jade, blue jade, orange jade, yellow and brown jade.

4. CHAKRA POWER

Jade symbolizes the user's intellectual energy and works best when worn in the heart chakra.

5. SPIRITUAL BENEFIT

Jade is a protective crystal that helps accept life's changes. It also helps shape the ideology. In addition to focusing on work, wearing jade also promotes duty and productivity. Jade also helps to harmonize and nurture inner strength.

6. PHYSICAL USE

Jade is known as a powerful crystal that teaches the lessons of life. It also activates the hyper adrenal glands, kidneys, bones, joints, skeletal system and reproductive system of our body. It balances body fluids, relieves spasms, and effectively treats anorexia.

7. EMOTIONAL INFLUENCE

Wearing jade can help you feel irritated and self-loathing. By increasing emotional intelligence, Jade conveys self-confidence, and exhibits suppressed emotions. Jade is an ambitious crystal that also supports you to have the courage to decline your life.

8. **AFFORDABLE SOLUTION**

One of our bestselling 100% natural jade eggs (3) is perfect for Kegel exercises and love vibrations!

IN A NUTSHELL

Crystals of love are known to be ideal for encouraging passion and vitality. If you don't want pink, red, or scarlet, use a delicate love stone like the best-selling Reiki Rose Craft. In addition to true love passions, love stones help nurture compassion, compassion, and care.

CHAPTER 4: GUIDE TO EXPAND MIND POWER

MAKING THE MOST OF YOUR CRYSTAL

Here you will find different ways to enjoy using the benefits of crystals.

TOUCHSTONE

Put your favorite crystal in your pocket or purse. Whenever you feel the need for an energy boost or want to focus your energy and attention on something special, you can hold it. How comfortable is it to have your favorite crystal at hand?

WEAR CRYSTAL

You may want to wear your crystal daily for support and energy balance. An easy way to do this is to put the crystal in a small pocket or pouch around your neck. You can also use the small wire cage as a pendant to carry. Wearing crystals as jewelry melts their energy into the aura and creates a delicate balance of body and emotion throughout the day. Use your intuition to pick jewelry just like any other crystal.

FOLLOWER

It causes crystals typically to be transported across the heart or thymus, controlling the immune system and strengthening the energy field.

EARRINGS

Crystals balance the yin and yang energy of the mind.

Bracelets and rings, worn on the left side, balance the energy we receive. Carried on the right side, it balances the energy we give or send.

NECKLACE

These are worn to improve your communication skills, especially to put your feelings and emotions into words.

PROGRAMMING

An effective way to use a crystal is to program its energy into a target of your choice. It requires you to focus your thoughts on the crystal, so that power goes with you to help you reach your goals. In this regard, the crystal must first be washed. Next, we need to do everything entirely and visualize our goals as clearly as possible.

Hold it with your right hand and place your right hand on your left. Focus on the visualization of the target and imagine it projected onto the crystal by a spiral of intense white light. It is an important step, and success depends on your commitment and the energy you transfer to the crystal. You can also speak your goals directly to Crystal.

This process may need to be repeated for several days to reach a big goal. However, if you wear or wear crystals, you can program several times a day to focus on your specific daily goals and tasks. Remember, as if the crystal possibilities are endless!

CRYSTAL LOOK AND FORTUNE TELLING

Natural light sources such as sunlight, moonlight, and candlelight allow you to see deep inside the crystal. The longer and deeper you look, the more you will discover its beauty and knowledge. It also helps relieve tension and revitalize personal well-being as well as become a focus of intuition.

CRYSTAL MASSAGE

Most crystals can be used directly for massage on the affected or sensitive area, or full body massage. Many are specially shaped and sophisticated for this purpose. The power of crystals relieves tension and pain.

CRYSTAL HEALING

The basis of crystal repair is the interaction between the intrinsic properties of crystals and the forces and properties of the human body. Your success depends on a simple flow from one to the other. Each crystal has unique features that make it suitable for use in certain diseases. An all-round treatment can be achieved by using a transparent crystal oscillator.

CRYSTAL SHAPES AND STRUCTURES

The following are a variety of crystal structures and shapes, and some of the critical applications that help in the selection.

SINGLE POINT OR GENERATOR: The sixth page will end someday. This is the focus of crystal energy, and these natural shapes come in different sizes.

DOUBLE TERMINATOR: There are points on both ends. The second point occurs when the crystal separates from the base early in its life, or when it forms on the soft earth. They are much rarer than single-point crystals, projecting energy from both ends, creating a uniform energy field.

It clusters a stunning combination of different sized dots and a joint base; it is especially useful in group locations such as meeting rooms and family rooms. Here they help create balance and harmony. Clusters often show an impressive display of shape and color. Collections are ideal for cleaning and recharging other crystals.

DEMANDING GENERATOR: Improved by clever grinding and shaping points for a more focused flow of energy. These crystals respond well to programming.

CRYSTAL ROD: provides a smooth end that can use for massage and a tip that can focus the crystal energy on a specific area. These are currently available for many types of stones.

PYRAMIDS: Focus your energy on crucial points and create ample space and meditation work. Especially useful when one side is facing north.

BALLS: Transparent crystal balls are traditionally used to the media, and other sensitive people can see them. They can help you see the past, and sometimes the future. It can also use almost any type of crystal or stone.

EGG: a traditional Chinese format that represents our essence and origin, it can be used as a mirror to reflect and focus your inner surface.

HEARTS: Polished crystal hearts are a perfect gift, symbolizing personal and universal love. It can be used not only for meditation and programming but also for strengthening the spirit.

DISCS: Large stones are often sliced to reveal their internal beauty and shape. These are great exhibits. Agate is widely used and is ideal for visual meditation and eye healing. There is a feeling of protection and warmth. It is also very suitable for cleaning and loading other crystals.

CABOCHONS: these smooth oval stones are usually set in jewelry. It is also ideal as a healing stone when used in a full crystal layout.

SOME CRYSTALS AND HEALING STONES

AGATE:

Agate is the foundation for ensuring physical, emotional, and intellectual balance. Agate works slowly, but it is sturdy. It also has the power to harmonize yin and yang. Agate gently builds self-acceptance and self-confidence, along with mental growth and emotional stability. The Northern Territory Agate brings happiness and color to users and helps their creativity.

AGATE AUSTRALIA:

Australian agate is very earth and a stone of the planet. It concentrates and stabilizes physical energy quickly, balancing emotional and intellectual energy.

AMAZONITE:

It aligns and balances the flesh and the ether body. Other than this, it also soothes nerves, promotes creative expression, and soothes emotions. Amazonite also brings joy, clarity, and an understanding of universal love.

AMETHYST:

Amethyst is known as the stone of peace and promotes spiritual wisdom. It has a calming effect and is ideal for meditation and improving mental skills. Amethyst is very protective and inspiring. It radiates God's love and promotes concentration.

BAND AMETHYST:

Band Amethyst is perfect for supporting all kinds of reflective tasks and meditation. Use it to get rid of resistance, get rid of change, get rid of negativity. The zonal amethyst creates a powerful healing field around the user.

AMETRINE:

Ametrine is a powerful combination of amethyst and citrine. It connects the physical realm with higher consciousness. It soothes and protects in vitro experiences and reduces psychological aggression. Ametrine combines the energy of men and women.

AMAZONITE:

Aligns and balances the flesh and the ether body. Amazonite soothes nerves, promotes creative expression, and soothes emotions. Amazonite also brings joy, clarity, and an understanding of universal love.

ANGELITE:

Angelite is a stone of consciousness and a symbol of peace and fraternity. Angelite facilitates contact with angels. Tell the truth and accept it with more compassion.

APACHE TEARS:

Apache tears absorb negative energy. Apache Tear relieves sadness, provides insight into the cause of need, and alleviates long-term illness. It promotes forgiveness.

ARAGONITE:

Aragonite is a reliable earth healer and foundation stone. It is useful for overworked people as it helps during times of stress and teaches patience and acceptance. Aragonite promotes discipline and credibility and combats anger and emotional stress.

AQUAMARINE:

Aquamarine provides emotional and intellectual stability, clarity, and inspiration. It helps in self-expression and calms the nerves. It also helps to eliminate fear, doubt, and phobia.

ASTROPHYLLITE:

Astrophyllite is an excellent stone for promoting in-vitro experiences. It boosts self-esteem and happiness. Astrophyllite gives you a better understanding of who you are and helps you get a complete picture of your personal and global transformation.

AZTEC STONE:

Aztec Stone helps you communicate with your guide.

AZTEC ROYAL PURPLE:

Aztec Royal Purple is also known as Purple Chalcedony. It absorbs negative energy and removes it from the body so it cannot be transmitted to others. Royal Aztec is also used to help people with bad dreams.

AZURITE:

Azurite leads to psychological and intuitive development. It pushes the soul to enlightenment. Azurite is a powerful healing stone that combines an understanding of the mind and body with the effects of thought and emotion on the body.

AZURITE MALACHITE:

Azurite Malachite creates flexibility and action flow. It refreshes and brightens your outlook. Azurite malachite helps to eliminate narcissistic traits while dispelling imagination, arrogance, and vanity.

BAND AGATE:

Band agate provides protection and security with stability and integrity. It will help you explore new areas and unique creativity, paying close attention to details.

BLACK TOURMALINE:

Black Tourmaline is the most powerful stone for negativity, chiefly protection for people. Jealousy. It is also a strong foundation.

BLOODSTONE:

Bloodstone is a powerful, healing stone that activates and improves both mind and body. Bloodstone conveys wisdom and sensitivity to inner guidance. It is also used to neutralize toxins and cleanse the blood.

BLUE AVENTURINE:

Blue Aventurine is a powerful spiritual healer. It helps you to speak to your heart by sincere means.

BLUE RACE AGATE:

Blue Race Agate supports verbal communication. Blue lace agate cools and soothes. It brings deep peace and helps to reach very high spiritual places.

BLUE KYANITE:

Blue Kyanite activates the higher chakras and the spirit that connects you to your life path and your true calling.

BOTSWANA AGATE:

Botswana Agate helps in artistic expression. It is an excellent healer for reprogramming cellular memory. Botswana agate helps in finding solutions instead of handling problems.

BRONZITE:

Bronzite promotes performance, politeness, and an equal attitude towards everyone. It strengthens determination.

CALCITE:

Calcite purifies the environment of negative energies and increases your strength. Calcite calms and fights idleness.

BLUE CALCITE:

Blue calcite enhances memory, intelligence, and concentration. It lowers blood pressure and relieves pain at all levels.

GOLD CALCITE:

Gold calcite is ideal for meditation and adjusting to higher mental levels. Its reason in the physical realm, while giving mental alertness.

MANGANO CALCITE:

Mangano Calcite is a forgiving stone. It causes fear and sadness. It helps to accept unconditional love, promotes healthy sleep, and prevents nightmares.

ORANGE CALCITE:

Orange calcite is a powerful and protective stone. It is an energy booster that boosts your body's vitality and conveys a definite meaning. Orange Calcite has powerful energy and cleansing properties, removes negative and stagnant energy, and brings shine and joy to your life.

CARNELIAN:

Carnelian is the stone of happiness and hope. It helps the courage and power to continue. Along with this, it also creates emotional balance and eliminates confusion.

CATSEYE:

Catseye stands for happiness, prosperity, and happiness. It stimulates your intuition. The Cat's Eye raises mental awareness and protects from negative energies.

CELESTITE:

Celestite is full of sacred energy. This stone is the teacher of the new era. It invites you to enlightenment, promotes purity of mind, and attracts happiness.

CHALCOPYRITE:

Chalcopyrite helps absorb mental knowledge. It is a compelling power line. It supports accurate perception and logical thinking when listening to your inner voice, helping you to be self-respecting and self-aware.

BLUE CHALCEDONY:

Blue Chalcedony is a creative stone that opens up new ideas and situations. It promotes a bright mood and the ability to look optimistically forward.

PINK CHALCEDONY:

Pink chalcedony is a spiritual stone that promotes empathy and inner peace and creates a deep sense of trust. Pink chalcedony promotes friendliness, creates a childlike wonder, and a desire to learn new things.

WHITE CHALCEDONY:

White Chalcedony conveys the feeling of compassion and generosity. Remove hostility and turn melancholy into joy.

CHAROITE:

Charoite is a soul stone, a transformational stone that overcomes fear. It provides deep physical and emotional healing. Besides this, it gives strength and spontaneity, reducing stress and anxiety.

CHIASTOLITE:

The ancient "cross-stone" Kiastolite was used to prevent malice and curse. As a powerful protection stone, it turns conflict into harmony. It provides answers to mysterious events.

CHRYSANTHEMUM STONE:

This stone teaches how to maintain a childish, innocent, and fun spirit. Chrysanthemum stone strengthens personality and overcomes prejudice, ignorance, self-righteousness, jealousy, and gaps.

CHRYSOCOLLA:

Chrysocolla is a gentle and sustainable stone. It cleans the house and the environment. Furthermore, it also promotes the internal harmony of the individual and gives pleasant energy to the relationship. It helps stabilize the home environment.

CHRYSOPRASE:

Chrysoprase increases flexibility. It sharpens mental clarity. Chrysoprase not only provides calmness but emotional, psychological, and physical health. Reduce critical attitudes and teach forgiveness.

CITRINE:

Citrine is known as the Stone of Abundance and Wealth. It's a powerful cleanser and regenerator. Citrine is fun, warm, and inspiring. Increases self-esteem and stimulates mental focus. It absorbs, transforms, dissipates, and grounds negative energy.

DALMATIAN STONES:

Dalmatian stones help get into your body from your head. It is a fixed stone that stimulates playfulness. Be cautioned here, and avoid over-analysis and move reflexively into your life.

DUMORTIERITE:

Dumortierite helps maintain youth and is ideal for developing a positive attitude to life. It enables you to stand up for yourself and adapt to the current reality.

EMERALDS:

Emeralds are stones of inspiration and endless patience. It promotes domestic bliss, unconditional love, and loyalty, unity, partnership, and friendship.

EPIDOTE:

Epidote provides the courage to enjoy your life and realize your dreams fully. Along with this, it also strengthens your sense of identity.

FLUORITE:

Fluorite manages, promotes, and improves the concentration of the mind. It is a calming stone that has a stable impact on all levels. It also enhances memory and concentration.

GARNET:

Garnet is a stone of passion, courage, and dedication. It stimulates the senses and increases vitality and endurance. It is also a stone that gives and regenerates powerful energy. Garnet is a stone of purity and truth, and inspiration for love and compassion. It balances libido and soothes emotional dissonance.

GREEN AVENTURINE:

Green Aventurine removes, rejuvenates, harmonizes, and protects the heart chakra. It is an all-round healer that brings happiness and emotional calm. Green Aventurine balances male / female energy.

HEMATITE:

Hematite is grounded and protected. Great for improving mental capacity and reducing stress. Hematite dispels negativity and promotes optimism.

HEMIMORPHITE:

Hemimorphite supports communication with the highest spiritual levels. It is a stone of personal responsibility that promotes acceptance and trust for your situation. Hemimorphite teaches you to create your reality.

HESSONITE:

Also known as green garnet, hessonite helps open intuition and mental capacity. Communicate self-esteem and eliminate guilt and inferiority.

HOWLITE:

Howlite is a charming stone. It is an excellent antidote to insomnia. Howlite prepares the mind to connect with the spiritual dimension and absorb wisdom and insight. Howlite teaches patience and helps eliminate anger and uncontrolled anger.

HYPERSTHENE:

Use Hypersthene for meditation and get immediate answers to your questions. It helps you face the right things in your good composition. Suitable for maintaining a healthy business relationship.

IOLITE:

Iolite is known as Sight stone. It is the activator of the third eye and stimulates a connection to inner knowledge. It assists in

Shamanic ceremonies to help travel outside the body.

JADE:

Jade is a symbol of purity and tranquility and enhances love and compassion. It is a protective stone that protects the wearer from damage. It is believed to attract happiness and friendship.

NEPHRITE JADE:

Nephrite Jade is used by Maori as a talisman to form a barrier against attack and disease. You should bless what you touch.

WHITE JADE:

White Jade supports decision making and emphasizes the best results.

JASPER:

Cleaning the internal organs can be grounds, protection, and deepening the fertility of your life.

BRECCIATED JASPER:

Brecciated Jasper is excellent for keeping your feet on the floor and emotionally stable.

LEOPARD-SKIN JASPER:

Leopard skin jasper reduces anxiety, heals the emotional body, and strengthens the sense of individuality. It produces the respect of indigenous people and the wisdom and healing of indigenous people.

OCEAN JASPER:

Ocean Jasper enhances creativity and originality. Help new ideas flourish.

POPPY JASPER:

Poppy Jasper stimulates a positive and fun attitude and motivates and energizes you to be creative. As a protective stone, it helps improve physical endurance, grounding, and balancing.

RED JASPER:

Red Jasper enables you to remember your dreams. Cleans and stabilizes the aura. Create an excellent "worry pearl" that calms your emotions as you play. Red jasper can support male sexual function.

RAINBOW JASPER:

Rainbow Jasper is a powerful protective stone that has a sedative effect and provides stability and security. It helps balance the emotional energy of the body.

STARRY JASPER:

Starry Jasper is an excellent protection and a foundational stone. It conveys wholeness, tranquility, and concern. Along with this, it also supports mental clarity and function.

SNAKE LEATHER JASPER:

Snake Leather Jasper protects you from the temptations that are harmful to you. It gives the environment a uniform and stable energy.

ZEBRA JASPER:

Zebra Jasper is a must. It allows you to focus on higher spiritual works on earth while providing protection, awareness, and insight. Zebra Jasper helps keep you away from your head.

JETS:

Jets use negative energy to relieve irrational fears. The plane is a guardian stone. Protect yourself from violence and illness.

LABRADORITE:

Labradorite is a mysterious stone and a light source. It increases awareness, enhances telepathy, and stimulates magic. It also enhances happiness and joy and gives a sense of security. It also relieves tension and pressure.

LAPIS LAZULI:

Lapis Lazuli expands consciousness and intelligence and improves mental abilities. Protects overcomes depression and promotes creative expression.

LAPIS MALACHITE:

Lapis malachite quickly reduces stress and brings deep peace. Easily absorbs negative energy and pollutants. Lapis malachite stimulates enlightenment and mental capacity. Especially useful for restoring the neck chakra.

LEPIDOLITE:

Lepidolite keeps you uplifted, balanced, and protected from depression. It reduces stress and negativity. It relieves allergies and strengthens the immune system.

MALACHITE:

Malachite boosts both positive and negative energies and takes mental energy to the planet. Malachite absorbs negative energy and protects it from radiation. A rock of change that promotes change and calculated risk-taking.

MUKAITO:

Mukaito (Australian Jasper) conveys both the desire for new experiences and the deep calm they face. It also Promotes versatility.

MOONSTONE:

Moonstone is a new beginning stone. Calms emotions. It promotes intuition and perception. Moonstone enhances the character of women. It also relieves instability and stress.

RAINBOW MOONSTONE:

Rainbow Moonstone connects with planning your entire life. It helps you intuitively read symbols and synchronicity and opens spiritual gifts.

MOSS AGATE:

Moss agate is stable and strongly tied to nature. You can see all the beauty you see. It has benefits for everyone involved in agriculture or botany. The Wealth stone also attracts richness.

PINK MOSS AGATE:

Moss agate brings general abundance, success, prosperity, and also helps to find peace with extreme or excessive duty in life.

It is a stone of compatibility and friendship. Moss agate is said to bring confidence and higher self-esteem and is also a protective stone.

MUSCOVITE:

Muscovite is a mysterious stone with a powerful angelic contact that stimulates a higher sense of self. Muscovite stimulates unconditional love and acceptance, while at the same time enabling the discovery of the human error.

AQUA OBSIDIAN:

Aqua obsidian stimulates the heart and neck chakras so that you can talk to the heart and understand the communication from the heart. Aqua obsidian can be used to increase mental awareness and support energy transfer.

OBSIDIAN:

Obsidian is a volcanic glass. Black obsidian is an excellent foundation stone as it shields against negative energies and dispels the unloving thoughts. Obsidian focuses on your inner vision, serves shamanic purposes, and is well suited for creative activities.

BLUE OBSIDIAN:

Blue Obsidian is a protective stone for physical and astral travel and also supports orientation skills. It affects neck chakra and improves communication skills, especially when learning a new language.

GREEN OBSIDIAN:

Green Obsidian balances the heart chakra helps loosen any bonds that others have placed on you and protects you from unwanted attachment in the future. This beautiful stone enables the self-realization of the importance of connecting with nature, love, tenderness, and care.

MAHOGANY OBSIDIAN:

Mahogany Obsidian drives growth in all areas and provides strength where needed. Use it to revive your life's work, fulfill your aspirations, and remove energy blockages.

RAINBOW OF SIDIAN:

The Rainbow of Sidian is a stone of joy and joy while protecting and grounding. It helps expand your awareness, sharpen your senses, and dig deep into mysterious phenomena and experiences. Rainbow of Sidian brings light and love to your life.

SILVER SHEEN OBSIDIAN:

Silver Sheen Obsidian is an ideal crystal for viewing crystals. Gives patience and patience, as needed, with lifelong benefits.

SNOWFLAKE OBSIDIAN:

Snowflake obsidian is an excellent way to balance the time of change. It helps remove the blockage by absorbing negative energy and activating self-strength.

BLACK ONYX:

Black onyx reduces stress and promotes self-regulation. Black onyx also promotes happiness, happiness, and more fabulous inspiration.

WHITE ONYX:

White Onyx helps you experience leadership and leverage your instincts.

PINK OPAL:

It is a stone for renewal that accompanies you in the path of your life. Pink opal teaches love and non-violence and nourishes every aspect of development.

DENDRITIC OPAL:

Dendritic opal promotes growth. It can be used to develop organizational skills, both mentally and physically.

PERIDOT:

Peridot was once used to protect people from evil spirits. It is still an aura protection stone. It is a powerful detergent that releases and neutralizes toxins at all levels. It helps you understand your destiny and your spiritual purpose. Peridot helps bring about the necessary changes by promoting growth.

PETALITE:

Petalite is known as the "Angel Stone" because it improves communication with angels and brings peace and tranquility. Useful for spiritual connection.

PETER SIT:

Peter Sit is said to dispel the illusions that help to recognize the beauty of the soul, including the "key to heaven." Peter Sit inspires decent power and loving instruction.

PETRIFIED TREES:

Petrified trees provide physical energy and relieve emotional pressure. It helps you stay in balance, take root down, and increase your connection with nature.

PICASSO STONE:

Picasso Stone supports the development of creative talent.

PRASIOLITE:

Prasiolite brings appreciation, awareness, and awareness to its users. Promotes recognition of achievements and facilitates their completion.

PRENTICE:

Prentice is recognized as an unconditional love stone. It also relieves nightmares, phobias, and deep fears. It helps to increase energy and provides protection also.

PYRITE:

Pyrite is a very protective stone that blocks or protects you from the negative energy of people, places, and things.

CLEAR QUARTZ:

Clear quartz is the world's most potent all-around healing and energy amplifier. Strengthens and cleans the power of other stones.

BLUE QUARTZ:

Blue Quartz can reach and hope others.

GOLDEN QUARTZ:

Golden Quartz (or Yellow Quartz) clarifies decision making and improves memory and concentration. Golden Quartz helps with nervous fatigue and burnout.

GREEN QUARTZ:

Opens and stabilizes the heart chakra. It transforms negative energy and stimulates creativity.

SNOW QUARTZ:

Snow quartz brings luck. It is also a calm stone. Snow quartz is useful for meditation, observing the contents, and for cleaning.

STRAWBERRY QUARTZ:

Strawberry quartz stimulates the heart and nurtures affection. We guide for you to enjoy every moment. Strawberry quartz also balances the connection between the physical and subtle bodies.

CRACKLE QUARTZ:

Crackle Quartz is a pure crystal that, when heated, is colored to a bright color. Kids especially love the bright colors of crackle quartz. With all the colors of crackle quartz, you can make a cheap chakra kit for kids.

RHODOCHROSITE:

Rhodochrosite helps relieve emotional pain resulting from unconscious memory and helps heal emotional wounds and trauma. It enhances memory and intelligence.

RHODONITE:

Pink enhances love, and black provides emotional protection. It gives you mental peace, builds trust, and reduces confusion.

RHYOLITE:

Rhyolite is an excellent stone that anchors you in the present, rather than looking back. It's good to find a solution. Rhyolite helps people who are lonely and often withdrawn and put others into their lives.

BANDSTEIN:

Bandstein is the stone that connects you to Mother Earth. It reveals your true nature and helps you to explore past illusions.

ROSE QUARTZ:

Rose Quartz is known as Love Stone. It balances emotions, heals them, and rejuvenates them. Cool your hot heart and eliminate accumulated anger, guilt, and jealousy. Rose Quartz promotes compassion and harmony.

SERENITE:

Serenite brings clarity. It delivers deep peace and is ideal for meditation and spiritual work.

SODALIS:

Sodalis streamlines and supports clear thinking, thus bringing clarity and truth. It creates an emotional balance. It helps to relieves panic attacks.

SONNENSTEIN:

Sonnenstein is a fun stone. It makes yourself happy and strengthens intelligence, desire, self-esteem, and optimism.

TIGER EYE:

The Tiger Eye brings happiness and optimism. Help reduce stubbornness. Promotes a positive attitude toward life and fosters self-esteem. It helps release unwanted emotions. The Tiger Eye raises awareness of Mother Earth.

BLUE TIGERS EYE:

The Blue Tigers Eye, also known as the Hawkeye, is soothing and also relieves stress. Blue Tiger Eye supports communication.

RED TIGER'S EYE:

Red Tiger Eye overcomes lethargy and provides motivation.

TIGERS IRON:

Tiger Iron is a combination of Jasper, Tiger Eye, and Hematite. Tiger Iron is a creative and artistic stone that creates unique talent.

TURQUOISE:

Turquoise is a promoter of self-fulfillment. It helps creative problem solving and calms the nerves when speaking in public. It stabilizes mood swings and brings peace of mind. Turquoise is an excellent stone for fatigue, depression, or panic attacks.

UNAKITE:

Unakite is the stone of vision, balancing emotions and spirituality. Unakite gently relieves conditions that impair mental and psychological growth.

CHAPTER 5: ENHANCE PSYCHIC AWARENESS WITH THE POWER OF CRYSTALS AND HEALING STONES

Then considering possible emotional causes of physical condition, it is often tough to generalize such relationships to make an overall assessment. Indeed, it can be challenging, as the appearance of a particular pathology is unique anyway. There are various possible causes of a specific condition. As a result, all suggested reasons discussed on the following pages are only available suggestions or presented as incentives to consider if there are similar circumstances or experiences in the actual case (or, of course, that It is the opposite!). So, if you have a better understanding of why you are sick or repeatedly suffering from illness, you should look into this information in more depth. On the other hand, if you feel confused or something is wrong, ignore it.

The term "this emotion" refers to an unconscious reaction that occurs without the consciousness of the current knowledge. The cause of these reactions can be related to specific goals and intentions, emotional background (previous experience), or mental attitudes (belief, opinion). However, they can all be summarized as "emotional." After all, they are usually all unconscious in some way and can only be understood or revealed after a thought-based severe self-examination.

You can't change it without consciously investigating reactions and mechanisms! It is also the reason why so many things always happen to us (they slip through our consciousness) and repeatedly cause unconscious mechanisms and physical illnesses. On the other hand, diseases are much less likely to occur due to conscious problems. The exception is the combination of consciousness and unconsciousness. Known issues affect our overall attention, allowing unconscious issues to continue its pace. However, in general, awareness-raising is a healing process. Mainly because we want to change the conditions of which we know.

When trying to put all this together into a simple formula that everyone can understand, the following concept emerges.

You may need therapeutic help here. The following individual entry suggestions are also vital in raising awareness. However, always follow the recommendations above. Don't worry if a particular reference doesn't make sense and doesn't cause a specific "a-ha!" Reveal experience.

There may be other causes besides the above. The best practical application is always the one specified in the entry, with a description of the individual crystals and their effects. The references given are based on experience, but should only be considered as suggestions or possibilities. Nevertheless, there are several ways to reach the same conclusion or result.

ABSCESSES

An Abscesses is a swelling of the skin that is rich in pus. They are the consequences of the body's natural way of fetching dead cells and toxic substances to the surface. Sometimes they are linked with high temperatures, and they are an essential part of the body's healing process.

Always consult a specialist, especially for abscesses that develop with symptoms of fever, because ulcers may be an external sign of deep-rooted intrinsic inflammatory disease. Also, with large ulcers, there is a risk of sepsis (blood poisoning).

If your abscess is recurring, especially in anxiety and severe emotional upset, you're concerned about how difficult it is to manage in life, how difficult it is for you, or how much you prefer to do so. It is useful to think about things. As if it doesn't exist, that is, "deny." Helping to resolve or address these problems can reduce the tendency for abscesses.

A proven home remedy for ulcers is the use of cold herbal packs in addition to the following crystal therapies.

Amethyst helps the body break down toxic waste products from inflammation, and the abscess quickly shrinks and disappears. Place a stone, section/slice, or whole crystal on the body. Apply Hildegard to the amethyst water of Bingen in the affected area. Or take Gemstone Essence (3-7 drops three times a day) to reduce the tendency for abscesses.

Heliotropes are useful when ulcers suddenly appear, and fever develops rapidly. Yellow-spotted crystals (traces of pus) are incredibly helpful. Place the fallen stone or cut/slice on the sore or take the gem essence (3-9 drops, three times a day).

Heliotrope can be used as an immediate remedy, but seek professional help immediately.

Ocean Jasper stimulates the dissipation of abscesses and reduces the inherent tendency to form in general. Crystals with lots of small brown spheres surrounded by green are particularly useful.

If acute, place stones or flats/discs on the affected area. Ocean Jasper can be worn for a long time (up to a few months) as a bracelet, necklace or pendant. Alternatively, you can drink gem water (200-300 ml of water during the day).

ABRASIONS, SCRAPES, AND GRAZES

Scratches are generally damaged to areas of the skin which are caused by skin surface contact or scratches. Although they often bleed a little, they can be more irritating and create a very unpleasant burning pain that damages the sensitive nerve endings of the skin. Also, there is an infection and pus formation. Especially if there are scratches and the area is dirty. Minimal bleeding is not enough to wash away dirt and bacteria. Therefore, abrasions should always be treated quickly with a medical disinfectant before covering the wound-large areas of abrasions that may require treatment by a specialist physician.

Similar to cutting, if you are well aware of the incident that caused the wear, you can use an iterative process to improve your condition and to heal more quickly.

Repeat the event, which made it necessary to wear at the location of the incident, as it occurred, as soon as possible after the incident occurred (of course, without injury!). Sometimes the whole thing needs to be repeated several times until the pain suddenly increases and then decreases. It is the stage where you have to stop. It is a consciousness-raising exercise that draws necessary energy attention to the affected areas and accelerates the healing process.

If the above method is not possible, obsidian can be used. You can pick it up with one hand or put it near the scratch to meet the condition

Impact the cells. Wounds can also be rinsed with diluted gem essence (10 drops in 100 ml of clean water) or obsidian gem water before applying plaster or bandage.

Rhodonite or Mucaite is suitable as a supplement in the form of tumble stones or discs, or as gem essence (5-9 drops) or gem water (100 ml), in addition to abrasions. Necklaces and pendants made from Rhodonite and Mookaite also support the healing process.

ACNE

The term includes several different skin disorders associated with adipose tissue accumulation, inflamed swelling, and pus-filled eruptions. The most common cause is acne vulgaris (also known as juvenile acne). It often occurs in adolescence and usually disappears by age 30.

Hormonal changes cause adolescent acne, but it is also exacerbated by high-fat foods, sweets, coffee, and nicotine. Covering acne with cosmetics is often as harmful as over-rinsing the skin with commercial soap or alcohol solutions. Therefore, if you want to reduce the number of acnes, eat low-fat foods, and want to know some names such as candy bars, eat and use only skin care products that do not contain soap and alcohol.

But crystal therapy only makes sense if a sensible diet and gentle skincare are done at the same time and are supplemented at the same time.

AMETHYST

It cleanses the skin. Hildegard von Bingen amethyst water is highly recommended.

CHRYSOPRASE

Stimulates detoxification and excretion of toxins and thus relieves skin problems. Place Stones or gemstones polished every night on the liver.

Otherwise, wear it as a bracelet, necklace, or pendant for a long time. Alternatively, it can be taken as gem essence (5 drops, three times a day) or gem water (10 ml, three times a day).

Moonstone regulates and coordinates hormonal changes during adolescence. Wear it for a few months, either as a pendant or, better yet, as a necklace or bracelet.

Rhodonite prevents the formation of open areas and acne scars when placed on the affected area in the form of flat, tumbled stones or pieces/discs. Long-term wear as a bracelet, necklace, or pendant also prevents the emotional stress that acne can cause.

ALLERGIES

Allergy is an acquired hypersensitivity to certain substances in and around the environment. Allergies tend to develop with repeated exposure to irritants and can manifest in several ways:

- rash
- Skin inflammation (dermatitis, eczema)

- Swelling and secretions of mucous membranes (hay fever)
- Airway disorders (allergic bronchial asthma)
- Extreme cases of anaphylactic shock. Blood pressure drops rapidly, and you lose consciousness. It is a life-threatening situation.

In addition to the last condition, all cases of severe allergic reactions deserve an immediate call for an ambulance or emergency medical care!

The prevalence of allergies is increasing rapidly as our organisms contain more and more toxic substances that cannot be used or excreted. Contamination and hypersensitivity to certain foods, of course, play essential roles. Other factors include stress, inadequate rest, and sleep. It is all overwhelming, overwhelming the body's ability to regenerate. As a result, an "allergic" reaction occurs.

A healthy diet, a toxin-free life (as good as you can today!) TVs, computer monitors, microwaves, electric pylons, etc. can help.

In particular, the diet should be professionally and, optionally, checked for individual tolerance limits. Rest, adequate sleep and regular detoxification (such as colon cleansing and fasting under expert supervision) also contribute to the body's need for regeneration. Finally, focus on what you may be allergic to emotionally.

Self-help treatment strategies for allergies are limited. But considering the cases like hay fever, crystals are beneficial. In more problematic issues, consult an expert-always under challenging situations or life-threatening situations such as anaphylactic shock.

Aquamarine helps many allergies, significantly when they are exacerbated by psychological or emotional pressure. It can use for respiratory reactions (from hay fever to bronchial asthma) and severe acute circulatory disorders. Aquamarine brings emotional lightness and relaxation.

Amber helps allergies that primarily affect the skin and mucous membranes. In any case, it should use when a particular contact has a specific dislike.

Blue lace agate stimulates the flow of lymph and quickly alleviates allergic reactions. Cleans the body and cures allergic symptoms. It also facilitates conflict management, promotes appropriate emotional responses, and eliminates allergies to specific situations.

Chrysoprase helps with allergies that occur after poisoning (or side effects of certain drugs) or due to a lack of food. It also alleviates sadness, jealousy, and allergies, which are by-products of peace of mind.

Landscape Jasper cleans tissues contaminated with toxins and waste products and helps with allergies. Relieves tension and awakens. It also relieves stress and strengthens motivation and assertiveness.

Ocean Jasper helps cleanse the body and regulate the immune system, especially in the bright areas of green/white inclusions or pure chalcedony. It reduces allergic reactions quickly and, in the long run, reduces the essential tendency of allergies.

Wear long like all crystal bracelets, necklaces, and pendants above. Alternatively, you can take gem essence as a supplement (3-7 drops, three times a day). Or use gem water for a long time (chewing 200-300 ml daily).

ARM AND LEG PAINS

Leg and arm pain are the most common side effect of colds, flu, and other febrile illnesses. They are caused by antibodies caused by the body's immune response, as well as bacterial metabolites and waste products. It reduces the supply of nutrients, stimulates nerve endings in tissues, disrupts blood circulation, and causes lymphatic fluid to accumulate. Usually, such pain is not a severe or dangerous symptom and often disappears spontaneously. Still, it can be quite uncomfortable at this point.

The combination of zonal chalcedony, magnesite, and amber is very effective in reducing such pain. Chalcedony promotes lymphatic flow, and magnesite relieves pain. Bernstein supports metabolism and boosts energy supply to tissues.

Moss agate, ocean jasper, or sardonyx also perform well when worn as an anklet or bracelet. All three belong to the group of chalcedony minerals, which helps in the entire healing process and cleaning and regenerating the body. It also prevents recurrence, and the cleansing effect quickly relieves leg and arm pain.

ARTERIOSCLEROSIS

Atherosclerosis is a thickening process of the arterial wall, which is the first protein and clotted blood, then fatty substances (such as cholesterol) and calcium deposits. It significantly reduces blood flow to specific organs, especially the heart and brain. Also, there is a risk of spontaneous thrombosis. It Completely blocks a blood vessel by a blood clot. It, in turn, can lead to heart failure and embolism.

Atherosclerosis begins slowly and insidiously. The first symptoms are Calf pain during walking (indicates poor blood circulation) Cold, colorless, bluish limbs. Sudden heartache; diminished physical, memory and concentration problems; dizziness; headache; sleep disorders; irritability; readily visible emotional issues.

An animal protein-free diet is an integral part of treating arteriosclerosis. Also, the menu should include foods rich in vitamins (especially vitamins C and E), adequate exercise, sleep, and time for general regeneration. Treatment should always be under the supervision of a specialist, as various background diseases and conditions can cause arteriosclerosis.

Three crystals, in particular, had a positive effect on the treatment.

Aventurine promotes detoxification, which prevents deposition on the arterial wall. It also prevents vessel inflammation and blood clots, reducing the risk of deposits that can lead to vessel narrowing.

You can wear it as a bracelet, necklace, or pendant for a long time. Also, try gemstone essence (3 drops, three times a day) or gemstone water (200-300 ml, small portions throughout the day).

Diamond breaks down deposits in blood vessels. Put a small raw diamond in 200-300 ml of water a day and drink the next day.

Heliotropes prevent further deposition in blood vessels. Especially useful when blood vessels are inflamed.

You can wear it as a bracelet, necklace, or pendant for a long time. Also, take as Gem Essence (5-7 drops three times a day) or Gem-Water (1 drop of 200-300ml throughout the day).

ASTHMA

The term "asthma" (also in Greek "dyspnea") includes various types of severe shortness of breath, from chest compressions to severe shortness of breath. The background depends on diseases such as cardiac asthma and asthmatic bronchitis.

In a more specific sense, bronchial asthma is considered an allergy and can cause by some suppressed skin condition. Here we describe this type of asthma.

Bronchial asthma has characterized by the tightness of small bronchial muscles, swelling of the mucous membranes, and dyspnea due to the excretion of thick, transparent "goosebumps" during exhalation. It leads to a severe case of shortness of breath. If this continues, it is a particular emergency, and you need to call an ambulance!

In this state, the air that should have exhaled collects and cannot inhale. It causes a deficiency of oxygen, which in turn leads to essential lung and heart function decline, which directly affects blood circulation. During an asthma attack, the latter effect manifests itself in the form of cold limbs and bluish lips, with a significant risk of subsequent complications due to damage to the heart.

It is worth noting the fact that allergies cause bronchial asthma, but it has different physical and mental properties. Attacks of asthma are caused not only by allergies such as pollen, house dust, flour, mold spores, chemicals but also by cigarette smoke, fog, physical stress, fear, anxiety, and other stressful situations. It will be triggered.

As a result, both the physical and emotional causes of asthma attacks need to investigate.

Worry and fear can cause chest tightness and impair the natural respiratory rhythm.

Asthma attacks can also be life-threatening, so professionals need medical supervision of all types of treatment. Crystal therapy, as a complementary therapy, can also alleviate seizures and reduce their incidence.

Apophyllite is the crystal of choice for acute asthma attacks. It has a relaxing effect on bronchospasm and acts as an expectorant, so it quickly relieves shortness of breath. Both green and transparent variants have this effect. However, green tourmaline has proven to be the most reliable.

Rutile quartz is the second-best crystal choice. Strictly speaking, it is suitable for the treatment of asthmatic bronchitis, but the two diseases are similar and therefore have a beneficial effect on bronchial asthma. It is especially true in the long run.

Tiger Eyes and Turquoise alleviate asthma attacks. The tiger's eye shape, called gold crystal, is especially recommended for the treatment of acute attacks.

For all of the above crystals, press the crystals firmly onto your chest, especially if they are sharp.

Wear rutile quartz in the form of a necklace or pendant on your chest between attacks. Apophyllite is gypsum-fixed or is usually only available as a crystal cluster so that it can pocket.

ATHLETE'S FOOT

An athlete's foot, most causes are considered to be external. The risks of fungal infections in public swimming pools and wrong shoes are evident. It is true that shoes with good foot hygiene and no "excessive humidity" reduce the risk of developing an athlete's foot. Despite this complaint, the internal environment of our body fluids is a much more critical factor.

Fungal infections, in particular, can only build a scaffold on the skin, mucous membranes, or tissues if the body already contains large amounts of toxic substances. Therefore, the disinfectants used in the pool can be harmful. Thorough cleansing with a skin-friendly drug is much more useful as a preventive and curative treatment.

However, the long-term solution is only guaranteed by complete detoxification. Effective home remedies such as ointments and crystals below from a 10% solution of tea tree oil only relieve annoying symptoms. Of course, their use remains fully justified. But without a diet or other detoxification precautions, no permanent cure can be obtained.

The combination of chrysoprase and smoky quartz is effective in controlling an athlete's foot, as detoxified chrysoprase and soluble smoky quartz importantly complement each other.

First, take Gem Essence Chrysoprase (5-7 drops, three times a day) or Gem-Water (20-100 ml, take a small amount in a day). At the same time, regularly place stones on the affected area. After 2-3 days, wear a smoky quartz necklace or pendant. This treatment should take several weeks, after which the results will be displayed. The detoxified chrysoprase and the melting smoky quartz complement each other in a meaningful way.

BACK PAIN

There are many possible causes of back pain. When transient, the reason is usually tension in the muscles of the back, which is caused by stress, poor posture, or lack of exercise. Apart from that, spinal problems, inflammation, side effects of other internal complaints, and even mental stress can lead to back pain.

In connection with the latter, guilt is often translated into shoulder pain. Also, the pressure to perform and emotional conflict develop as pain in the upper back (around the thoracic spine). Sexual problems and emotional stress can occur as sacral and coccyx pain, but similar lower back pain can be caused by financial anxiety.

However, these are just some of the possible causes. Since the back and spine are synonymous with the "straightness" of physical and psychological postures, in principle, any type of stress or concern can lead to similar pain.

When treating back problems, we should be attentive towards both physical and emotional causes. Treatments that consist only of treatment of symptoms, such as massage and crystal therapy, provide relief in a short time only if the actual emotional or psychological cause remains untreated. Therefore, a professional physical examination is always recommended for all forms of persistent low back pain with a heavy emotional burden, along with other types of treatment.

Kunzite helps with back pain caused by compression of the nerve by a herniated disc or sciatica. Relieves pain and relaxes the affected area. Massages and chiropractic treatments can be given without harmful side effects only when the area is completely relaxed. Kunzite emotionally promotes commitment and humility, while at the same time remains true to itself. It is precisely what the spine means, as it needs to support the spine and stay flexible.

Place crystals or stones directly on the painful area-or use gem essence (5-9 drops, three times a day) or gem water (100-200 ml per day).

Magnesite helps relieve tension in the back and upper neck. It is especially useful if the pain is due to pressure, or if future conflicts are expected. It leads to patience and enhances our ability to withstand all kinds of mental or emotional stress.

For best results, wear a bracelet, necklace, or pendant on your back. You can also take gem essence (5-7 drops, 3-5 times a day) or gem water (200-300 ml, swallow throughout the day).

Smoky quartz helps with all kinds of back problems. It relieves tense muscles and helps to achieve a better posture. It also produces a calm sensation under high stress, enhancing its ability to withstand pressure and stress. More extended wear also reduces the inherent tendency to stress. The crystals or stones are to be placed in the painful area. Or wear it as a necklace or pendant. Or you can take gem essence (5-7 drops, 3-5 times a day) or gem water (200-300 ml, small portions throughout the day).

Ruby is primarily useful for lower back problems-wood areas, sacrum, coccyx. When faced with complex concerns, it also has been shown to bring courage and strength to help many with sexual problems and anxiety.

Place or attach crystals, discs, and stones on the sacrum. Or wear it as a necklace or pendant.

Emeralds can assist people who have back ailments. They arise when they lose their directional sense or mainly suffer from dishonesty, tensions, feelings of failure, and fatigue.

It can also be used if only some indirect effects on the back of the affected area. Such as inflammation of the intestines and other organs) are involved.

They place (or fix) crystals, sections/disks, or tipped stones in sensitive areas. Alternatively, you can take gemstone essence (3-7 drops daily, 3-5 times daily) or gemstone water (200-300 ml droplets throughout the day).

Black Tourmaline relieves all kinds of back pain and reduces all types of stress and emotional stress. For the most effective results, place the crystal face down and fix it in the painful area. If actual tourmaline crystals are not available, then a suitable alternative is cut/slice or tumble stone.

Obsidian, used with tourmaline, is especially useful for pain emanating from clearly identifiable points.

A piece of fallen obsidian (preferably the so-called "tear of Apache" shape) is placed in the painful area. Place four tourmaline crystals on the outside. Obsidian relieves pain, and tourmaline crystals give off excess energy.

BEDSORES

Pressure ulcers are a painful area of skin damage caused by pressure and circulatory disorders, which, in advanced stages, can reach tissue layers as deep as the bone. They often occur in patients who need to stay in bed for a long time and can no longer turn around themselves.

As the condition progresses without treatment, deeper layers of tissue are affected and, in fact, in severe cases, penetrate as deep as the bone. Four stages of progression usually classify pressure ulcers, and the overall process affects tissues that begin to die without adequate nutrient supply. The so-called first degree involves the local redness of the skin and muscles. The second degree consists of the formation of bubbles. Next, the deep open wound of a third-degree wound is followed by inflammation of the bone marrow as a fourth-degree pressure ulcer.

Even the first degree is often worse than it seems! Pressure ulcers can extend deep into the surrounding fatty and muscle tissue.

Additional exacerbating factors associated with pressure ulcers include overweight (too high pressure). Underweight (lack of natural pads), fluid retention (edema), moisture, high temperature, lying down, anemia, diabetes.

Preventing pressure ulcers and treating first-degree cases requires consistent pressure relief. The patient's lying position is changed at least every 2 hours and, if possible, physically moves. Depending on which part of the body is affected, a unique air-filled rubber ring, and a particular mattress can be placed on the bed where the patient can lie down. Bedding is smooth and wrinkle-free and requires skincare (no creams that clog pores), a balanced diet rich in vitamins and enzymes, and clean water (gentle detoxification). In the case of incontinence, do not allow persons to lie in a moist bed for a long time. In all cases of pressure ulcers, you should seek professional help in the form of a doctor, naturopath, or nurse. The sooner, the better. If the pressure ulcer is more than one, treatment is essential.

Depending on its severity and severity, the healing of pressure ulcers is supported by many crystals. However, this additional treatment requires specialized medical attention. Older home remedies that have proven to be effective recommend spring and raw eggs under the floor to prevent and treat pressure ulcers. The results are even better if you use pure water and organic eggs instead of tap water and battery-powered eggs. It sounds strange. Please try it anyway. There is no harm.

Amethyst is especially advisable when cleaning the affected area with Amethyst water from Hildegard von Bingen (first degree only) or when water can be taken internally (10 ml). Supports pressure sore skincare three times, several times a day, no more!).

Carnelian, garnet pyrope, and rose quartz improve blood circulation in the affected area and reduce the risk of pressure ulcers. However, do not use it at high temperatures or if it is already infected (because it may cause adverse effects).

However, Rhodonite and Mucaite are the primary crystals associated with pressure ulcers. As crystals that promote wound healing, they also stimulate the healing process of pressure ulcers. However, open wounds (such as third-degree wounds) need to be regularly and carefully cleaned during this process.

Emeralds can be used as a supplement when a bone is already affected to suppress bone marrow inflammation and relieve pain.

For such items, place the raw crystals around the bed or in between the bed frame and the mattress. Wear as a bracelet or necklace as needed, unless there is an increased risk of pressure ulcers and lying problems.

However, one of the easiest ways is to take gem essence (3-7 drops, three times a day) or gem water (100-200 ml in small tins during the day) internally.

BED WETTING

Bedwetting at night is usually not a physical cause, especially in children. Instead, it is more emotional, mainly because of fear, personal loss, jealousy (to younger siblings), or sensory anxiety in the child (e.g., after significant changes in family and environment). Also, natural Earth's radiation fields and electromagnetic pollution are thought to lead to urination during sleep. If the problem persists, then all these causes should be investigated and resolved.

In contrast, adult incontinence, H. Involuntary urination due to reduced bladder control. It can be caused by bladder infections or disorders, pelvic hernia, neuropathy, benign prostatic hyperplasia, and weakness of the pelvic floor muscles. Other causes include chronic anxiety, feelings of anxiety, or a loss of control of your life (or part of it), but they tend to be unclear. Therefore, every professional medical examination should include both the latter aspect and the physiological cause.

Amazonite's help bedwetting concerning sadness, failure, and durable resistance. Very restless children, who tend to develop faster emotionally than intellectually, also respond positively to Amazonite therapy in this context.

Chrysoprase stops bedwetting very quickly, especially in children. It relieves jealousy and a lack of care and helps children rediscover their safety. As a mineral of chalcedony, it strengthens the bladder.

Citrine is especially useful for incontinence caused by weak muscles in the bladder and pelvic floor. Also, it helps enhance self-confidence and regain control of your own life.

Heliotropes help incontinence caused by severe concerns, loss of control over one's life, or incontinence after cystitis and related illnesses.

Wear crystals as bracelets, necklaces, and pendants for all of the above purposes. Alternatively, or place the glass directly on the bubble area and stick it in place with a bandage. If necessary.

If none of these work or bedwetting is caused by cystitis or a weak bladder, try the crystals described below for bladder problems.

BLADDER PROBLEMS

Bladder problems can be classified in two ways. The first is a weak bladder that is prone to infections, frequent urination, and possibly incontinence. The other is a bladder with a disease that suppresses urine.

Bladder weakness is often caused by a general lack of vital energy and is often associated with fear and life difficulties. Here, you may lose control of your immediate situation or certain parts of your life. The result is often an inflammatory bladder with urine retention. The latter is a kind of repulsion, trying to use extreme measures to control things.

Of course, inflammation can also cause the bladder to be diseased, but the presence of weaknesses makes it worse.

All cystitis should be treated professionally. Progression of infection from the urethra to the kidneys can lead to dangerous complications.

The Agate with bladder characteristics is especially with a pink spot in the middle-is particularly suitable for the treatment of chronic and acute cystitis. It also increases emotional stability and facilitates crisis and problem resolution.

Place the polished crystal, section/disc on the pubis, or wear it as a pendant.

Aquamarine helps with a weak bladder, frequent urination, and incontinence. It helps control bladder function and other lifestyle issues.

There is no direct physical contact, but it should be worn for a long time as a bracelet, necklace, or pendant. Or take as a gem essence (3-7 drops, three times a day).

However, garnet pyrope is the number one crystal for treating weak bladder and its associated infectious tendency. It also helps you deal with severe living conditions.

Place it on the pubis as a crystal or polished crystal. Heliotropes also help treat acute cystitis, which usually needs to be healed by rest. Don't count on me.

Heliotrope only-If used, place a section/slice or polished lens on the pubis and stay in bed.

Nephrite or Blue Chalcedony relieves urinary retention. Both crystals eliminate the need to keep everything and help maintain emotional "fluidity."

Place a stone on the pubis. Or you can wear it longer as a bracelet, necklace or pendant. Or take as Gem Essence (3-7 drops, three times daily).

Ocean Jasper helps with a weak bladder, acute inflammation, and urinary retention. The effect is best described as a regulation of bladder function. In severe cases, it helps emotionally and creates a sense of hope, optimism, the joy of living, a new force-as a result, life is much more comfortable.

Place the stone on top of the pubis or wear it for a long time as a necklace, pendant, or gem crystal.

BLISTERS

Blistering occurs as a result of mechanical pressure or friction (such as abnormal handling of tight shoes or tools). Crystals can achieve rapid healing. Do not blister as there is a risk of infection. Other well-known home remedies for blisters are Bach's life-saving drugs (water droplets on the bladder) or the comfrey leaf of a rubbing shoe.

Agate (with proper signature), Amethyst, Blue Chalcedony, and Ocean Jasper heal unblended blisters. The body reabsorbs the fluid in the blisters and renews the damaged skin layer. You can use Blue Chalcedony and

Ocean Jasper first to drain the liquid. Then apply agate to stimulate the exchange of dead skin layers. Finally, amethyst is used to reduce the sensitivity of the affected dirt. If you have only one of the above crystals, you can also apply each crystal individually.

Rhodonite is excellent for open or burst blisters. It relieves pain and accelerates the healing of public and sensitive areas.

Blue tourmaline is particularly suitable for stimulating water absorption from the bladder. Prevents the formation of bubbles even if they are placed where they were previously under pressure. The essence of gems applied to spots has the same effect.

Place the fallen stone or flat disc or piece of crystal on the affected area (or fix with a plaster). Then apply a few drops of a particular gem essence for effective in vitro treatment. If using amethyst, also use

Hildegard von Bingen amethyst water on the bladder.

Spirits containing ethyl alcohol (ethanol) should be diluted (10 drops per 100 ml of water) when used to treat blisters.

BLOATEDNESS

The more colloquial terms "bloating" or "bloating" are the names used for the sensations that are felt as a result of the increased formation of intestinal gas. This can occur with certain foods (beans, cabbage, etc.) or because the regular release of gas is blocked by constipation. If your gut flora is unbalanced or if you have other digestive problems, you may feel bloated for a long time.

Occasionally, a "mentally indigestible" situation or problem can lead to bloating. Also, it is due to a lack of exercise, especially when sitting at work. A careful combination of regular use (such as visits to the gym or daily walks), stomach massages, and certain foods (eating fennel, drinking caraway tea) is a proven treatment at home. It is one of them.

Agate also relieves bloating by regulating and matching the intestinal flora. Placing cuts/slices or tumble stones that contain evenly curved bands on the stomach gives quick results. Also, agate provides the essential and necessary emotional stability needed to tackle and "digest" unpleasant problems. However, the most effective is the agate, which is worn for a long time as a necklace or pendant.

Emeralds relieve flatulence of all kinds. Take it as a gem essence before meals (5-7 drops three times a day). Alternatively, it can be placed as a giant horseshoe on the abdomen. It can also be used to extend from the outside of the colon. Otherwise, wear for a long time as a necklace or pendant.

Black tourmaline is especially useful when bloating is associated with constipation. Use for emeralds as above. If you are forming horseshoe shapes from tourmaline crystals, make sure they point in the same direction as the flow of waste through the large intestine.

BLOOD CIRCULATION

Cardiovascular problems usually only occur when blood flow is compromised. Typically, the blood supply to tissues of different parts of the body depends on the needs of these parts of our organism. If more activity is needed, circulation will increase. Reduced activity slows blood circulation. Only in the event of an emergency does the blood flow decrease significantly, as the body secures a blood supply to the most important organs (brain, heart, liver, kidneys) and as a precautionary measure Need to limit blood flow. "Less important" organs and body parts. Examples of such emergencies include blood loss, high fever, or dangerous situations. Traditional Chinese medicine calls this regulatory system a "triple warmer."

If the triple warmer is affected or interrupted in any way, it can still be activated without the need for an emergency mechanism. Among other things, this can chronically cool the hands and feet. Alternatively, blood circulation can be compromised by low blood pressure, a weak heart, or narrowing and blockage of blood vessels (arteriosclerosis). Malnutrition (too much fat and animal protein), smoking, and certain types of drugs (always read all drug and drug package instructions and instructions) can lead to such criticisms. Therefore, detoxification and switching to a healthier diet are some of the most important precautions when dealing with cardiovascular disease.

A slight circulatory disorder is manifested by a sensation of coldness, numbness or tingling in the limbs, increased tiredness, pain caused by anxiety, and dizziness under certain circumstances. Continuous circulatory disorders can be dangerous. It may damage organs and tissues. Therefore, the crystals mentioned here are intended for use only when there is a slight disturbance in blood circulation. If the disorder occurs repeatedly or if it lasts for a long time, you should seek professional advice.

Garnet pyrope is the most important crystal for both general and local problems. Garnet strengthens the triple warmer, ensuring that the energy is evenly distributed throughout the body. Thus, it helps in case of rapid onset of fatigue, coldness, pain caused by general stress.

Place a crystal or polished crystal on the affected area for local improvement of circulation. Generally, if circulation is poor, wear a necklace or pendant or take gemstone essence (3-5 drops, five times a day).

Obsidian is especially useful for chronically chilled hands and feet, even if parts of the body are "fallen asleep" or if smoking blocks the arteries in the legs.

If possible, hold the crystal in your hand and put one (cabochon) on your shoe, or place the crystal on the part of your body that has poor circulation to secure it.

Rhodochrosite stimulates blood circulation. Like garnet, it has a positive effect on blood circulation. Do not use rhodochrosite if it is much faster than garnet and tends to have high blood pressure.

Wear a necklace or pendant, or take small pieces of gem essence (3 drops, three times a day is enough).

Rose quartz is suitable for localized circulatory disorders. If the affected area becomes cold, tingling, or feels "sleeping," massage the whole thing with a rose quartz ball or polished crystal.

BLOOD PRESSURE

Causes arterial blood pressure two factors: blood volume pumped from heart to artery causes of resistance to the system and its flow because of the elasticity and state of the blood vessel and blood wall's liquidity. The narrowed arteries and the blood of "mucus."

Blood pressure, slack in dilating arteries, and the blood that "flows easily."

It decreases blood pressure. Usually, blood pressure increases rapidly due to physical activity: breathing, stress, or dangerous situations. Blood pressure tends to drop when you are calm and relaxed, especially when lying down

Below or under the influence of drugs), or you are taking certain medications.

However, persistent high or low blood pressure can cause problems, some of which are very serious.

HIGH BLOOD PRESSURE:

High Blood pressure, also termed as hypertension Fatigue, headache, and other manifestations energy levels the condition can cause heart and kidney problems or neurological disorders.

To eliminate these instances, if severe visceral disorders cause such symptoms, avoid more severe complications, high blood pressure should treat professionally only. So always ask your doctor signs of high blood pressure occur.

The symptoms of hypotension include:

Fatigue, weakness, dizziness, pallor or cold skin, and fast but weak pulse. It also tends to be faint or "black." "Out" or pass out.

As with hypertension, you should seek professional medical help as soon as possible to find out the cause. Changes in blood pressure many different emotional symptoms State that makes it almost impossible to give real general advice. Surely, just help decide a person.

Background causes high blood pressure and tension, stress or excitement-and equivalent relationships between low blood pressure and deficiency energy, loss of consciousness, and laziness.

May you need to ask personal or related life problems or anything that may cause them. Do you have any symptoms?

Many crystals increase or decrease blood pressure. However, their practical application is that they are physical, Emotional causes clarified at the same time. Regular animal protein-free diet fasting and other detoxification measures should always be related to the treatment of blood pressure too high or too low.

High blood pressure here is some crystals you can use contact with medical advice and receive treatment professionally.

Amethyst immediately lowers blood pressure.

Saw the saucer gently (Like a brush) -without touching Body-Forehead to Top Head, neck, back, towards the legs and arms floor. People if your blood pressure drops sharply and symptoms such as dizziness appear, you can stabilize your blood pressure compensatory exercise on the body (up the central axis of the body starting from below the front-above and the head. This treatment provides a soothing and relaxing effect physically and emotionally.

Blue chalcedony lowers blood pressure in the long run. Not very suitable for short-term relief, but ideal for long-term relief stabilization of "normal" blood pressure. Lapis lazuli sinks very fast unless it affects blood pressure. It contains traces of pyrite (fool's gold)! The best blue and white spotted lapis lazuli is also suitable, particularly suitable calcite to reduce acute hypertension. That only uses it for a short time.

Sodalite also has a rapid drop effect.

It can use longer than blood pressure and Lapis Lazuli time.

LOW BLOOD PRESSURE

Similar supplementary normal medical can prove the following it's useful.

FIRE-OPAL:

Fire-opal also provides quick relief low blood pressure can help sudden attacks of dizziness or Loss of consciousness, e.g. "All when it gets up, it turns black.

Hematite stabilizes blood pressure continuously during low blood pressure or weakness, e.g. When the body overgrows or when you are alive through the difficult stages of life. Rhodocrosite causes blood vessels it contracts and increases blood pressure. That please use only for a short time low blood pressure—for example, lack of sleep. Ruby generally raises blood pressure to stabilize in the normal range.

Take the pair of crystals mentioned in your hands to achieve one rapid changes in blood pressure due to the circulation meridian (one of the 12 mains) Energy path of the body).

BREASTFEEDING:

The main reason for breastfeeding problems is usually the lack of rest and insufficient rest for breastfeeding mothers. In these conditions or situations, you cannot entirely focus on your baby. Taking rest is especially important in the early stages of breastfeeding, where everything is new, and there are no known routines. Do not underestimate a calm and safe atmosphere in the actual milk production process.

In particular, as soon as all urgent breastfeeding problems have overcome, especially the first milk flow and breastfeeding infection, further immediate breastfeeding problems may occur. For example, in the early stages, the ducts from the individual mammary glands to the nipple are relatively narrow, making it difficult for milk to flow, which can cause pain during the first milk production flow. In this case, it is convenient to glue white cheese shells with curd cream, massage, and use the following crystals. Breast infections, on the other hand, occur because bacteria can enter small cracks or crevices in the nipple. It can be prevented in advance by an active massage (pull, push) of the nipple during pregnancy. However, if irritation develops during breastfeeding, the heat shield helps prevent further deterioration. Card packs also provide peace of mind, and the crystals described below also have excellent results in healing teat infections.

The confused emotional relationship between mother and child is often due to breastfeeding problems. But from the beginning, this must be rejected with great empathy. Not only is this assumption wrong in almost all cases, but it is also useless in that in certain circumstances, it is a notion that it is a useful concept for guilty of a mother.

Of course, mothers breastfeed their babies. For most of the problems, it is worth considering the "mind care" of the mother herself. For example, if a mother takes care of others or ignores herself too much, breast inflammation is more likely. Besides, it is the actual stress caused by childbirth, and it is often the significant changes in family life that cause breastfeeding problems. Therefore, the EU needs to avoid inappropriate concerns and concerns for others.

Replace as much as possible by focusing on her health with breastfeeding mother.

Chalcedony is a very light blue, pink, or white without stripes, making it the perfect crystal for all kinds of breastfeeding problems. It relieves breast inflammation, increases milk yield, promotes initial flow into the passageway, and provides the safety needed for breastfeeding. After all, the white chalcedony has not called "milk crystal." It has been used for centuries to promote milk production and facilitate breastfeeding. All of the above chalcedony types can wear on your chest as a necklace or pendant.

BROKEN BONES

Crystals support the healing process as soon as the fractured bone is fixed with splints. However, make sure the fracture is set correctly before using it.

Apatite, in particular, stimulates the healing of fractured bones-when used effectively; deformation can occur if the bones are not correctly adjusted, which can cause long-term problems. Therefore, use apatite only if the x-ray determines that the bone is in the correct position, and this is medically confirmed.

Apatite promotes fracture healing to this extent, so parts grow together twice as fast as usual. It is believed that this is because apatite is chemically a type of calcium phosphate and, therefore, is so similar to the composition of human bone that it can trigger the corresponding growth impulse.

Calcite is also not as reliable or effective as apatite, but it promotes fracture healing. It stimulates calcium metabolism and has a positive effect on bone growth.

For both apatite and calcite, place or attach stone or crystal as close to the break as possible. Unfortunately, gypsum casts are often an obstacle, but they also contain healing chemicals, primarily calcium. Therefore, the use of Gem Essence is recommended as an additional treatment (5-9 drops, five times a day) or Gem water (a small amount of 200-300 ml during the day).

The same is true for crystals that relieve pain and those that heal bruise and damaged tissues and nerves.

Kunzite, obsidian, or sugilite are additional crystals that help accelerate the healing process of bones and relieve pain. Rhodonite helps heal bruise.

Tourmaline should be used when nerve damage associated with numbness or temporary paralysis symptoms is also suspected.

BRUISING

Bruises occur when blood vessels are damaged or torn, and blood flows into connective tissue, muscles, or limbs. Causes are usually severe blows, dislocations, sprains, fractures, or (less frequently) simple pressure points on the body. The skin covering the bruise is initially bluish. Then later, the reddish dye in the blood, a greenish yellow-hemoglobin, is broken down. Bruising usually disappears within a few weeks, but proper treatment can save time. Common home remedies include applying cold packs and arnica cream to the skin and ingesting homeopathic arnica preparations.

Rhodonite and obsidian crystals, in particular, help promote rapid bruise recovery, relieve pain, and overcome shock from painful injuries.

Place or secure (with a bandage) a flat, tumbled mineral or disc/section on the affected area. If necessary, put it in your existing dressing.

Precious metal essences (5-9 drops as needed) or gem water (100-200 ml per mouth throughout the day) can also help.

BRONCHITIS

Bronchitis is a bronchial infection that often develops as a complication of a cold. It affects the two main branches of the trachea and the second branch that leads to the lungs. The complications of the original disease are often caused by clogging of the tissue with toxic substances, from dairy products. Many cows are now bred for the mass production of milk and dairy products. As a result, milk, which currently lacks enzymes and is rich in antibiotic residues and other harmful substances, is challenging for humans to digest. It, in turn, leads to an obstruction of our tissue. Such "contamination" interferes with the activity of the natural immune system and thus increases susceptibility to infection.

A simple cold can develop into bronchitis relatively quickly. It first appears as a cough, causing mucus (especially in the morning), elevated body temperature, general weakness, and occasionally chest pain and shortness of breath. Bronchitis attacks usually subside within a few days. Still, they always seek expert medical advice to ensure that your lungs become infected without you noticing them, and eventually, your lungs are not affected. Many home remedies have proven very useful when it comes to supporting the healing process. In particular, thermal envelopes made from potato, goose fat, or onions are folk remedies that have been tried and tested for prompt relief.

Bronchitis can be chronic with recurrent attacks and should be treated with extreme caution. The emotional background of the disease should also be considered. As with any cold, personal interactions with others and the environment also play a role. Also, some people may experience sadness and sorrow, especially with bronchitis-along with the profound effects of hidden fear they may have. The crystals described below adequately mitigate these effects.

Apophyllite quickly relieves acute bronchitis, supports full recovery from the disease, and stimulates mucosal regeneration. It also helps with shyness, anxiety, anxiety, chest tightness, and anxiety.

Ocean Jasper helps with both acute and chronic bronchitis. It relieves coughs and shortness of breath, regulates high temperatures and prevents dangerously high temperatures. It also strengthens the willingness to relax and gives hope and optimism.

Rutile quartz is equally useful for acute and chronic bronchitis. Opaque crystals with a lot of rutile threads are most active. Rutile quartz is emotionally brightening and antidepressant. It helps resolve hidden [unconscious] fears, maintain hope, and recover from stubborn illness.

Emeralds help with acute bronchitis and develop quickly, especially from a cold. In this way, the accelerated course of the disease is slowed down, and further complications are avoided. Emeralds also support a quick and complete recovery. Jewels are commonly used when bronchitis attacks are reduced and wholly cured and not chronic.

Use Apophyllite to place or adhere to crystals or small groups of crystals directly to the bronchial region.

For Ocean Jasper, Rutile Quartz, and Emerald, place or bond polished crystals to the bronchi, and wear a necklace or pendant for extended periods as needed. Gem Essence can be taken internally (5-7 drops, 3-5 times daily) or gem water (100-300 ml swallowed daily).

BURNS

Burns is called painful tissue damage caused by local exposure to temperatures above 50 degrees Celsius (about 120 degrees Fahrenheit). Open flames, hot gases, vapors, heated liquids, and objects can cause burns and burns, as well as the effects of electrical energy and radiation (ultraviolet rays, x-rays, microwaves, radioactivity).

Burns are classified into four degrees, depending on the depth and extent of the damage.

First-degree burns are characterized by swelling and painful skin that is reddish for several days.

Second-degree burns can cause blisters and, in significant cases, scarring. The blisters do not become damaged, rupture, or open because the risk of infection and scar formation increases exponentially.

A third-degree burn will destroy the entire skin. Ironically, the nerve endings themselves are also damaged, so these areas are often more or less painless. Such wounds heal very slowly from the periphery to the center, leaving a single scar. Skin grafts are usually needed to support the healing process.

A fourth-degree burn will also damage the underlying tissue. In most cases, complete recovery is not possible, which means permanent damage.

Severe burns and burns require immediate medical attention or immediate medical attention.

In other cases of burns, first aid is always to place the affected area under cold running water and hold it until the first severe pain subsides or stops. If hot liquids cause burns, remove wet clothes immediately. Then cover the injury and burn area with a sterile burn bandage or pad to make the wound visible to the doctor. When treating large areas of burns, you should also drink a large amount of liquid (about 1 liter of water mixed with 3 g of salt) to make up for the loss of fluid from the wound and prevent shock from burns.

For first-degree injuries or small second-degree burns, there is no blistering. Still, orange light irradiation, aloe vera plant juice treatment, St. John's wort oil, or wild mountain lavender ether oil (closed Only blisters!).

Blue tourmaline promotes skin renewal without leaving scars and can be used for second-degree burns. Take gem essence (5-7 drops every 15 minutes initially, then 3-7 drops every hour after that, 3-7 drops three times a day after the second day). If possible, soak the burnt area with cold water containing gem essence (20 drops in 1 liter of water).

Gemstone water can be used in the same way (up to 2 liters a day, by mouth). For more extensive burns, you can also soak the wound with this water before applying the compress.

Rhodonite should be used immediately or for first-degree injuries so that the wound can heal completely. Like blue tourmaline, it is used both internally and externally. For small burns, it is sufficient to moisten the polished crystals and keep them on the burned area.

CANCER

The general and general term "cancer" has used to describe a malignant tumor associated with tumorigenesis. These cells are mostly fatal if not treated properly and professionally.

Tumors result from the unregulated growth of body tissues. In contrast to the morphology of cancer, so-called "benign" tumors are most distant from the surrounding tissue and only replace them. In other words, they do not penetrate surrounding tissues or blood vessels and are only a problem if they occur in an unwanted location (e.g., the brain). In contrast, malignant tumors invade and destroy other tissues and blood vessels, causing metastases. These are accessory tumors that spread not only to the lymphatic and blood systems but also to various biological pathways. Commonly called cancers are these tumors and their effects.

When a malignant tumor develops, the properties of the original cells and their metabolism also change. In human life, every section is different and specific. It evolves according to the task and has unique functions. When such a cell becomes cancerous, it becomes a non-specific unicellular organism. It takes over the metabolism of all single-cell plants that live without oxygen and inherits a specific unicellular survival program that appears to be deeply rooted in our genes. In other words, its functionality and behavior are "duplication, duplication, duplication." Cells, like "social groups," leave the former "home tissue" and begin to divide roughly. Therefore, malignant tumors increase and begin to spread.

So why are cells threatening and falling into the old single-cell survival pattern? Of course, they contain chemicals that attack the cell's common genetic heritage. It is commonly called a carcinogen and includes pesticides, fertilizers, food colorings, additives, heavy metals, asbestos fibers, etc. You have a wide choice, and you can even add some medications. Others include cigarette smoke, excess alcohol, hormones in meat and drinking water, some viruses, and long-term inflammatory conditions. Radiation effects are especially causal, whether in the form of x-rays, technical radiation, other types of radioactivity, or natural energy in a particular area. When you're diagnosed with cancer, it's always a good idea to test where you live, work, and sleep.

However, it is not just external risk factors that can lead to tumor formation. There are also many internal (endogenous) factors. Parasites also cause cancer. Most people with many types of pests live in the system without knowing it and without necessarily causing problems. However, factors such as constant stress, chronic inflammation, and poisoning reduce the efficiency of the immune system, making it incapable of coping with certain types of parasites that attack specific cells. It continues to increase in speed (i.e., is absorbed by cells) and tries to deal with the situation by splitting faster. At first glance, this division process seems to be advantageous as it reduces the number of parasites per cell in half. However, there is an initial race condition that can lead to genuinely fatal results.

The cause of cancer has intensely debated for a long time in the general condition and lifestyle of the human body. It is an ongoing discussion (as explained above), as it is not easy to identify objects that are not obvious to the outside world. Nevertheless, there is little doubt that the constant stress of modern life has a "burning out" effect on our adrenaline production. As a consequence, it leads to a wither of the immune system, leading to a toxic buildup, whereby our metabolites can sometimes also play an important role.

In particular, there is a dangerous belief that the continued high consumption of sugar and flour leads to the fact that, in reality, the actual amount of sugar cannot process metabolically. As a result, the body's sugar storage capacity is exhausted. This problem can also cause so-called age-related Diabetes, which can lead to increased cell division and cells that adapt to sugar-consuming metabolism. It can be fatal for later survival.

As mentioned, our connective tissue is, among other things, space where non-drainable substances are "temporarily" stored. Unfortunately, modern eating habits and lifestyle habits are making these "shops" increasingly the ultimate storage location. Blocked by more and more waste. After all, they suffer from a lack of oxygen and nutrients and can no longer get rid of toxic waste. The effect is that the store will eventually starve and suffocate with its garbage! It's no wonder that some cell panics, at some point, goes its way, and begins an emergency survival program. The trust in the biological community has been lost, and the need for air, water, and nutrients are not countered. It's as if the cells decided to solve the problem themselves!

I am convinced that reducing stress, reducing sugar and flour and animal protein intake and diet, and Detoxification and metabolic regulation are the most important measures. Also, look closely at external factors such as radiation and pollution, where you sleep, where you live, where you work, and if you are wholly concerned about those factors. We recommend that you change it.

Of course, I understand that advocating such a philosophy can cause some very annoying problems. For example, what about your diet? Does the menu contain organic, lively, digestible, and live foods? It is in contrast to the so-called "fast food" mere fillings. What do you drink good water-what is a liquid full of useless substances like sugar, alcohol, artificial flavors, stimulants? How do we handle the body? How much rest, sleep, care, and beneficial activity do you provide? How much effort and effort do you need? How do you anticipate an unpleasant situation or complaint?

We believe these are the questions we have to ask ourselves more often. At least some illnesses, especially cancer, have to question a normal lifestyle. While the time for nutrition, sleep, and renewal is fundamental to life, all conditions that affect these pillars affect our work, leisure, the rhythm of life, habits, and vices, stress, frustration, and frustration.

Do we think we need to ask ourselves how we live, as a whole, part of the community, nature, the universe? Or will you act as an individual as if you are away from the rest of the world? When asking about our health, we ask ourselves, our home and family, our tendencies and interests, beliefs, beliefs, philosophy of life, hope and yearning, the joy of life, meaning of life, and much more. Ask failure to face a big face to our overall goal, how to pose a problem to success? After all, these things affect us all in our minds, souls, spirits, and bodies. Fine-tuned internal teamwork extends to individual cells and their survival efforts.

Therefore, I'm convinced that asbestos fiber, cigarette packs, and even our genes can't take full responsibility for causing cancer. Instead, I believe that all illnesses are the result of the development of diverse individuals based on their physical, emotional, and mental states. Not everyone agrees or agrees with this statement. Still, it is the "bad" cells themselves that are associated with radiation therapy, chemotherapy, and often the highly unwanted side effects of oncologists. Conversely, cancer cells are victims of derailed tissue in the body! The ability of tissues, lymph, blood, digestion, Detoxification, excretion, and regenerators should be supported as soon as possible so that they do not require a survival program for individual cells in the body.

What do you mean, here are only personal observations and conclusions? Therefore, these considerations are nothing more and, therefore, not based on the traditional medical profession or expertise. Nonetheless, I think it's correct to quote three observations I've made about all the people I know who have survived cancer and are in optimal health today:

1. You have undergone radical physical healing. Holistic treatment was consistent. The body was detoxified. Metabolism has been reorganized to take into account improved nutrition and care, tissue acidification, and colon treatment—excretion of toxic substances, homeopathy therapy.

2. Your attitude has become "more life-friendly." Harmful habits have been given up, regeneration (sleep and rest), strengthening, and training (sports and exercise) have become part of everyday life. And their rhythms have become more structured. Also, the living space, especially for sleep, living, and work, has been thoroughly inspected for adverse radiation and biological effects, and all necessary changes have been made!

3. The dispute is resolved by counseling or therapy. Critical and non-critical life problems often associated with changes in work, society, and relationships have been identified. The first goals of life were reevaluated-and. Finally, the lifestyle was adapted to the desire for happiness and the fulfillment of that desire.

Of course, it is as invasive as cancer, and there is no guarantee, depending on the type of cancer and its spread to the human body.

As with all illnesses, changing lifestyles and environments, and resolving emotional and emotional conflicts must be a positive step for everyone. (Latter-conflict resolution-it's especially crucial because it's often overlooked! Nevertheless, even in traditional medicine, the long-term smoldering conflict is a psychological consequence of long-standing smoldering conflicts in the body. It is known to be a seedbed, and the result may not be that the cell decides to survive by becoming "selfish" at one time?).

If we have cancer, we have to change our lives. By treating disease with the latest advances in medicine, surgery, radiation, and chemotherapy, we continue our lives, backed by competent and professional advice Natural alternatives There is a means, and there are treatments to achieve an overall cure.

Cancer is no longer the death penalty! Let's take as an example all those who have overcome it and enjoyed the best health today! The road to success is the guiding principle for how to deal with cancer yourself.

From this point of view, we recommend the following crystals. Crystal therapy and related treatments cannot cure disease. Instead, Crystals can make a valuable contribution to general well-being as part of an individually tailored holistic treatment involving the body, mind, and soul. And this should be beneficial to everyone in all situations.

Noble Opal reminds you of the original goals, colorful and creative ideas of your dream of life. In this way, we touch on important points and create a lot of contention from them. How do you want to live your life? Remember, the necessary changes will be visible. Opals also help regain enthusiasm and joy, and above all, the motivation to be healthy and healthy again. At the physical level, it ensures clean tissue and lymph, which improves the nutrition of cells and the removal of waste products from them.

Wear the bracelet, necklace, or pendant in close contact with your body, or place it in your area to be visible and close to your body. Also, take gemstone essence (3-9 drops daily, 3-7 times daily) or gemstone water (200-300 ml, sip slowly throughout the day).

Ocean Jasper is a healing crystal associated with tumors. Many of the variants have the characteristics of individual cells or "spherical and cluster-like" characteristics of cell populations. Being a type of chalcedony, it stimulates cleansing of tissues and lymphatic systems, strengthens cleansing, anti-inflammatory, and immune system. It promotes cell and tissue regeneration and regulates metabolism. In this way, it acts as the best "reorganizer."

Emotionally, it offers hope, the courage to live, and a desire for a new start. Under their influence, change is not a burden and necessary obligation, but a unique opportunity to be happy. It improves sleep and regenerative powers and accelerates many healing processes.

The crystal ring around the bed is thus particularly useful. Orange Jasper can be worn in the form of bracelets, necklaces, and pendants. It can be taken internally as either Gem Essence (3-9 drops daily, 3-7 times daily) or Gem-Water (200-300 ml teaspoon daily).

Green tourmaline contains metallic elements of chromium and vanadium, which have healthy detoxification, anti-inflammatory, and regenerative effects. Vanadium metal is remarkably durable in the denaturing process, in which case it follows the principle of "healing" to counteract the destructive cycle.

Tourmaline also improves energy processes and the flow of information in the body, so the affected cells are reintegrated into the organism. Also, it promotes the resolution of emotional conflicts, leads to a more positive attitude, improves general joy, and enables regeneration. After all, it also helps you find your way in a new life phase and redefines forgotten goals.

Most effective when worn as a bracelet, necklace, or pendant. It can also be taken as Gem Essence (3-9 drops daily, 3-7 times a day) or Gem-Water (200-300 ml, in small portions throughout the day). You can also place a green tourmaline slice/section in front of a strong torch and aim the beam at the affected area. This action will transfer the healing information of the crystal to the right place.

The latter treatment has a potent effect and should be slowly increased (three 5-minute sessions on day 1, three 10-minute sessions on day 2, etc.).

CARPAL TUNNEL SYNDROME

The carpal tunnel is located on the wrist below the bones and tendons of the wrist. The forearm nerves that control the flexible tendons of the fingers and the muscles of the thumb ball all pass through the carpal tunnel. Chronic inflammation of the wrist, sprain damage, and excessive tension or twisting can cause the carpal tunnel to narrow. As a result, the brachial nerve is trapped in the carpal tunnel. This causes coldness and numbness on the fingers, especially on the index and middle fingers. Then there are problems gripping and holding things, especially early in the morning.

Also, patients can experience arm pain at night, which can extend to the shoulders as well as hand pain and tingling. Gently massaging or shaking your hands can help, but in the long run, this is not enough. When carpal tunnel syndrome develops over a long period, the muscles of the thumb contract significantly.

Carpal tunnel syndrome is often caused by inflammation, especially with rheumatism. Another cause is a sprained wrist. Take an uncomfortable posture when writing or using your hands. It can also be caused by changes in the body balance associated with spinal problems.

Traditional medicine still believes in an unexplained carpal tunnel syndrome, so a holistic, specialized diagnosis is needed. If the cause is more rheumatic, the purification process is, of course, necessary (see also Detoxification and rheumatism). However, if the purpose is ergonomic, total body therapy is recommended (e.g., craniosacral therapy).

Of course, crystals help in both cases. Amazonite and green tourmaline are the most remarkable healing crystals of carpal tunnel syndrome. They support both the causes that are the result of inflammatory conditions and the consequences of overload. As lead-bearing feldspars, Amazonites help shrink many types of tissue, and green tourmaline stimulates the regeneration of pinched nerves.

Chrysocolla, heliotropes, emeralds, and turquoises are especially helpful when inflammation and rheumatism are the cause of the background. Also, it detoxifies the crystals. That is, the exact cause of the syndrome is also treated.

Amber, Dumortierite, Lavender Jade, and Sugilite help the result of sprains and poor posture, causing symptomatic mechanical narrowing of the carpal tunnel. Dumortierite is especially suitable in this case as it has a pain-relieving effect and removes terrible habits. It also balances the whole body and guarantees emotional lightness.

In either case, wear the bracelet directly on your wrist or attach a flat rough or tumbled stone with a linen bandage or similar binding.

You can also take Gemstone Essence (57 drops, three times a day) or Gemstone Water (200-300 ml, small doses daily).

CATARACTS

A cataract is a blur of the lens of the eye. It is caused by the body's waste (a form often referred to as aging-related), metabolic disorders (e.g., diabetes), prenatal infection, or gradual deposition as a result of injury, radiation, fever, blindness (lightning). It triggers poisoning and other eye diseases. Cataracts cause a diminished ability to focus and reduced vision, leading to complete blindness.

In conventional medicine, cataracts are treated by surgery in which the lens of the eye is partially or entirely removed and replaced with a lens implant, contact lenses, or cataract glasses.

In alternative medicine, where the use of healing crystals also plays a role, there are precautionary measures that can either stop the usually gradual progression of blurring or at least slow down this degrading process. Detoxification, metabolic regulation, and treatment of the underlying illness or injury are crucial challenges for such therapies.

Rock crystals have been used in cataracts for centuries. Especially useful in the early stages when the lens is out of focus. Place a small crystal or stone directly into the closed eye. Clear and bright, so-called "Herkimer."

Diamond is particularly suitable. The diamond itself will also help in later phases. If the cataract is due to the accumulation of waste, then its best effect can be achieved. Take Gem Essence (3-7 drops daily, 3-5 times daily) or Gem-Water (200-300ml daily, in smaller doses). Jewels can also be placed directly or between the so-called "third eye" eyebrows.

Obsidian can also be especially helpful in injuring results if you need to use it as soon as possible. Depending on the type of injury, place a flat crystal directly on the eye, or use an obsidian part on the eye without direct contact. Gently relaxing and looking at the mirror-polished area of this mineral will have another healing effect.

Emeralds help cataracts that result from metabolic problems. (In the broadest sense, poisoning and previous infections also belong to this category.) Place crystals on the eyes and liver (preferably at the same time). Also, wear a necklace or pendant and take gem essence (5-9 drops, 3-5 times a day) or gem water (200-300 ml, swallow throughout the day).

CELLULITE

Cellulite is the physical evidence of structural changes in the subcutaneous tissue, where fat deposits form and cause irregularities on the skin surface ("orange peel"). These skin changes have nothing to do with the actual health of cellulite, the inflammation of skin cells. Cellulite, like many skin and tissue disorders, is a cause that is often mistakenly described as being age-related, due to waste deposits and lymphatic buildup. The decomposition of such waste deposits and toxins has led to many crystals, such as Blue Chalcedony and Chrysoprase.

Exercise, a healthy diet, massage the skin, and alternating hot and cold water can help alleviate this condition. However, so far, only two crystals are suitable for the actual regeneration of skin affected by cellulite.

Ocean Jasper stimulates tissue regeneration and reorganization after an intensive detoxification course. Therefore, if the brown tourmaline (dravite) is not immediately useful, it can be used as a "preparation" before using the brown tourmaline (dravite).

Take gemstone water (rinse 200-300 ml throughout the day).

Magnesium-rich dravite tourmaline promotes cleansing and detoxification of connective tissue and deeper skin layers, as well as their structural regeneration. In this way, the fat deposits of cellulite dissolve, eliminating the small dents and bumps on the skin surface.

For this purpose, dravite tourmaline must be used in two ways. Take Gemstone Essence (3-5 drops, three times a day) or Gem-Water (200-300 ml drops throughout the day). On the other hand, Dravite crystals and boulders are placed on the affected part of the body. It concentrates on the effect in these areas.

CHILDBIRTH

Birth is a complex physical activity that involves a variety of emotional and psychological experiences that consist of a series of challenging stages. As a result, a wide range of crystals is needed to support the mother and child, mainly when problems occur.

However, it should be remembered that, despite efforts and pain, childbirth is an entirely natural phenomenon and is not considered a medical "problem."

Therefore, the use of crystals should be left in the background and used only when needed. The following table summarizes all crystals that support birth. By presenting the information in this way, it is expected that the appropriate crystal can be selected and used correctly.

BEFORE AND DURING BIRTH		
Crystal	**Effect**	**Practical applications**
Carnelian	Give strength and courage before birth	Wear as a necklace or pendant
Magnesite	Has a relaxing effect, eliminating resistance and birth crisis	Wear as a necklace or pendant, or take gem essence (7 drops) as needed
Chrysocolla	Has a relaxing effect and helps to expand	Wear as a necklace or pendant, or take gem essence (7

		drops) as needed
Heliotrope	Protect from infection	Take Gemstone Essence (5-7 drops every 2 hours if needed)
Biotite-Lens	Bring work; have a relaxing effect. Promotes easy childbirth	Hold it in your hand. Lying on the pubis to support contractions
Malachite	Stimulates contractions and relieves pain	Hold it in your hand. Place it on your pubic bone to help it contract. To

		relieve pain, take gem essence (7 drops) as needed.

IMMEDIATELY AFTER THE BIRTH

Crystal	Effect	Practical applications
Kunzite	Helps accept the role of child and mother	Wear as a necklace or pendant
Blue Tourmaline	In the case of sadness	Wear it as a necklace or pendant, or

	or emotional crisis	take on the gem essence (3-5 drops)
Epidote	Playback when used up	Wear as a necklace or pendant, or take gem essence (5 drops) as needed
Topaz	Help find my identity	Wear as a necklace or pendant
Blue or Pink Chalcedony	Promotes milk production.	Please use it as a necklace or pendant.

LATER POST-NATAL

Crystal	Effect	Practical applications
Agate	Helps the uterus return to normal size and condition	Place the rolled stone with the uterus signature on the body
Rhodonite	Heal wounds and cuts	Take Gem Essence first (three times a day, 5-7 drops). Then, when all bleeding has stopped, put the fallen

		crystal in your panties.
Pink Agate	For all kinds of inflammation	Place a tipped stone with a signature that looks like an inflamed area of the body
Moonstone	Helps change hormones	Wear as a necklace or pendant
Mookaite	Stabilize health	Wear as a necklace or pendant

CHILDREN

Crystal	Effect	Practical applications
Amethyst	Promotes the "arrival" of children in our world	Place the rolled crystal or small crystal on the child's bed.
Rutile Quartz	Helps overcome the trauma of childbirth	Place the rolled crystal or small crystal on the child's bed.
Calcite	For stable development	Place the rolled crystal or small crystal on

		the child's bed.
Aquamarine	Relieves hypersensitivity eczema	Place the rolled or small crystals on the diaper.
Citrine	Because of digestive problems	Place the rolled or small crystals on the diaper.
Emerald or Peridot	Stimulates the decomposition of bilirubin. Apply peridot only if the skin is very yellow	Place rolled crystals (peridot) or small crystals (emerald) on the diaper.

CIRCULATION PROBLEMS

Circulatory Disorders Blood flowing through veins and arteries is wholly or partially closed. It can cause this heart problem. Hypertension or hypotension (e.g., during pregnancy), hormonal changes (e.g., during pregnancy, menopause), infections, general weakness of the autonomic nervous system, or blockages or disorders of blood vessels the latter is notable.

Although the heart's work supports blood transport, sufficient elasticity, tone, and coordinated muscle arteries are also essential to transport the arteries for proper blood flow. The contraction of their muscles causes blood to be pumped out of the heart. Chinese herbal medicine very clearly formulates the relationship between the heart and the circulatory system as follows.

The center is the Emperor. The sound flow is his first formula to do the job and tragic to him. Emperors and officials play!

A thorough examination of inadequate blood flow usually shows certain phenomena such as deposits on blood vessels and their walls, stenosis or enlargement (varicose veins), and inflammation-these are the results.

Tissue with toxic deposits. Detoxification-Therefore, fiction is needed to avoid circulation problems (detoxification). A general diet-free diet rich in animal proteins and vitamins (especially C and E), adequate physical activity, rest, sleep, and regeneration time is appropriate precautions.

Cardiovascular problems often manifest as sudden changes in blood pressure and pulse rate. It then leads to inner fear, fatigue, pallor, dizziness, loss of consciousness, cold sweat, trembling limbs-in extreme cases-failure.

First Aid Immediately raises your feet and place your head in the cold water to resuscitate a person. However, professional medical advice and help should always try to determine the cause.

Problems often arise emotionally from stress and stressful situations. Internal disturbances and resistances seem to reflect the desires and intentions associated with blood pressure fluctuations. A sense of failure, overwork, and lack of energy are often present along with cardiovascular problems, lack of joy, and enthusiasm. Therefore, they often turn to personal goals and opportunities to rediscover their goals. And the new destination is still the best spirit of cardiovascular disease! Many crystals (blood pressure; see Heart Problems) described elsewhere can be used to stimulate or calm traffic. Therefore, the next diamond that stabilizes the circulation can have an impact.

Garnet pyrope traffic promotes blood circulation. The problem is that it can prevent the cycle from being interrupted (when used on time), and as a new metabolic crystal, it can also promote cleansing and improve vascular vitality. Emotionally, it helps overcome resistance, mobilize vital energy stores, and help patients.

Weakness, dizziness, brief seizures of the hematite, and tiger iron-especially when waking up early in the morning or because of pregnancy. Both crystals emotionally help you. Full of energy Tiger Iron in particular, quickly eliminates fatigue and poor performance. Ruby stimulates blood circulation and helps with fatigue, pallor, dizziness, colds, sweating, and trembling limbs. It can be used in time to prevent flow interruptions. Not only time but also passion and enthusiasm for emotion wear all the listed crystal necklaces or pendants on at least one waist. The crystal hangs above the pubis.

Tumble stone made of garnet pyrope, ruby, hematite, and tiger iron or glue with plaster. It is also possible to absorb the essence of gems, only in small amounts (2-4 drops, twice a day). The same is true for gem water (100 in a small sip of 200 ml daily).

COLD

So-called cold appears cough, classic symptoms of the head.

Colds and faintness, all common characterized as an influenza infection,

They do not have much in actual common flu. Chill in the head Cold as the name can be turned on.

Sometimes due to cold such exposure can weaken its mucosal immune defense structure Airway membrane. On the other hand, a hand that can spread anywhere already stressed the body, such as toxins and waste).

Most often, however, the cold is in the shape of the virus in which the tissue and cells are present infect the garbage that makes the infection spread and interferes with the activity of the immune system. Colds can generally be prevented by "exacerbating" the problem body. This includes regular exercise in the current form. In the air (any weather!),

Open windows that end the daily shower with cold water and proper detoxification.

Especially dairy products giving up how to increase the trend?

With colds, sore throat, bronchitis. Sinusitis further protection can also obtain through rinse bio and mouth and teeth, cold compress sunflower oil daily for 10-20 minutes. Do not swallow the oil under all circumstances, but spit it out. Then rinse your mouth with lukewarm water! This oil absorbs toxic substances and waste products and supports healing of a cold.

Direct airway cooling (e.g., When breathing through the mouth), indirect cooling of the whole body (Lack of clothes), and cold feet can play roles that cause the effects of colds. Cold the legs primarily cause a decrease in reflexes. Blood flow to the nasal mucosa. Therefore, viruses tend to occur mostly in the cold and wet transition phases and to a lesser extent. A dry and cold winter. Mainly summer cold drink with internal cooling.

Down effect and cold draft the critical role of the so-called "summer."

cold". But, as I said, the cold is a viral disease. The virus that already exists.

Mucous membranes or they have inhaled and exploited the actual weaknesses of the immune system and where they can be it spread very suddenly. Usually, this is caused by the catarrh and Mucous inflammation membrane. The immune system is often balanced. There are more stressful ones. The influx of bacteria that can continue leads to inflammation and formation pus. Fever is associated with cold, an essential part of my body defense- Should not be restrained with humanism early to avoid complications. Any next body parts and additional advertisement symptoms can consider severe complications:

- head cold

- Throat-cough, hoarse voice
- Bronchus-deep cough, breathing difficulty
- Lungs-weakness, loss of appetite, high fever, night sweats, shortness of breath
- Heart-acute heart disease
- Sinus-Aggravating pain
- Through pressure and prevention
- Middle ear-ear pain, fever
- Meninges-headache, vomiting

Sudden illness, tremors, disturbance of consciousness have a simple cold, cough, or wrinkle. It can quickly process with crystals. However, if the symptoms persist progression to other parts of the body, for example, towards the sinuses or bronchi, Doctor or naturopath consult. But again, the crystals can be used to complement secure surveillance and professional approaches treatment in the course of the disease, a successful cure. However, in most cases, healing has done by reversing the process original cause or direction of cause like many other illnesses. It is an excellent thought to be essential for a cold emotional background of illness-personal relationships, lifestyle, and environment, sadness, or depression (especially Cases of bronchitis).

CHAPTER 6: INCREASE SPIRITUAL ENERGY WITH THE POWER OF CRYSTALS AND HEALING STONES

ARE YOU ON A SPIRITUAL PATH?

Maybe you want to develop your intuition or like to learn to work with your guide? Or do you just want to be more in tune with your inner mind and experience the connection between mind and body at a deeper level?

Perhaps you are working towards a rising energy awareness in Kundalini?

Nature provides powerful tools that support us in our spiritual efforts, and these tools are pure crystals.

These high-vibration stones provide metaphysical benefits and help develop our mental talents and abilities. Let's look at some of these benefits and how to use pure crystals to improve your spiritual journey.

THE BENEFITS OF SPIRITUAL CRYSTALS & HOW TO USE THEM

SPIRITUAL CRYSTALS HELP CONNECT THE MIND, BODY & SPIRIT

To improve one side of your life, you need to enhance the other. It is impossible because our hearts, our bodies, and our hearts are the interwoven tapestries. There is nothing to represent itself because the aspects of the mind, body, and soul are intertwined.

When we have a headache, it is a physical symptom that often results from mental elements such as stress, which can often also have spiritual aspects. When we are happy, we are energized and connected to the world. When we eat poorly, we feel physically lacking in energy, but we are mentally depressed and challenging to connect intellectually.

These are just a few examples of how the connections of mind, body, and spirit work. It is essential to know that the problem will persist until the root cause of the problem is found. Physical symptoms rarely become physical.

Mental crystals help heal physical, mental, emotional, and emotional wounds.

Heart chakra stones such as Rose Quartz, Emerald, and Rhodonite are great for mental health and support us with a loving and gentle nature.

Lepidolite is the ideal stone for mental health as it eliminates stress, fear, and blurs the thinking. Amazonite helps reduce anger, and citrine brings luck.

About physical dissatisfaction, a little research will show which stones are useful in which areas of the body. For example, red jasper helps the cardiovascular system, rhodolite improves cold, and flu symptoms and yellow crystals help digestive health.

There are many stones known for their spiritual benefits. For example, Amethyst and Azurite help us to align our intuition. Rutile Quartz helps us achieve our spiritual awakenings and teaches us how Wright helps us connect with the spiritual world.

But these stones not only affect the physical, mental, or spiritual aspects of the body. For example, if a stone is known to help with mental health, it also disturbs certain physical and psychological aspects of health. Because spirituality and physical and mental health are inextricably linked, it is always best to choose a comprehensive approach to crystal healing. You can use individual crystals together to support yourself and heal the root cause.

SPIRITUAL CRYSTALS IGNITE THE VIOLET FLAME VIBRATION

Amethyst embodies the vibration of a purple flame, also called a purple ray. It turns the body's negative energy into light and love. This healing vibration is managed by the Ascended Master St. Germain, who lived in the 16th century and dedicated his life to healing others from their negative energies.

The vibrations of the purple flame help remove negative energy from the body and protect us from negative entities and psychological attacks. It can be accessed by holding Amethyst stones in the presence of Amethyst Geode or by wearing Amethyst jewelry and asking St. Germain for help.

Most purple rocks, such as Tanzanite, Purple Sugilite, and Purple Pearlite, have purple frame vibration, but amethyst is the strongest.

Amethyst has high-frequency vibrations that help us discover and access our spirituality more easily and quickly—placing these healing stones in the aura shifts the energy to higher frequencies.

SPIRITUAL CRYSTALS DEEPEN YOUR MEDITATION PRACTICE

Meditation is one of the most important things you can do when working to improve spirituality. It brings us closer to the higher self and facilitates the transition to a deeper state of consciousness. Meditation with crystals further enhances these results.

Meditation crystals help calm us, purify negative energies, remove chakras, improve your intuition, and guide us to spiritual guidance.

Amethyst is our favorite meditation crystal. It not only calms the mind, body, and soul, but it also helps the brain to speak quietly and connect us to higher consciousness. Other meditation crystals are clear quartz, chevron amethyst, ametrine, rutile quartz, azurite, labradorite, black tourmaline, and carnelian.

SPIRITUAL CRYSTAL CONNECT US TO HIGHER SPIRIT

Spiritual Crystals improve your connection with higher self, guides, angels, and God.

We all have different mental communication methods that are unique to us. Fluoroscopy is when you can see a guide or have a vision. Clairaudience is when you hear a paranormal talking. When you feel something in your body that helps you to know what it is. Claire's knowledge is when he just knows something, but not how he knows it.

Spiritual crystals help improve these and less natural methods.

Purple perlite and prehnite are excellent crystals for connecting and communicating with your guides and angels. They help us hear, see, feel, or know what they are saying to us.

Other crystals that are particularly useful in connection with high spirits are Rainbow Fluorite, Clear Quartz, Rainbow Moonstone, Angelite, Azurite, and Lepidolite.

SPIRITUAL CRYSTALS AWAKEN THE KUNDALINI

Kundalini's awakening occurs when Kundalini energy moves the spine from the base chakra to the crown chakra. The Kundalini snake is located at the base of the spine, and when it awakens and climbs into the crown chakra, it means the movement of consciousness toward enlightenment.

There are a variety of pure crystals that help Kundalini's awakening process, such as Shiveringham, Tiger Eye, Moldavite, and Red Jasper. Serpentine eliminates most of the illnesses and problems that can occur when waking the Kundalini.

HOW DO SPIRITUAL CRYSTALS RELATE TO THE CHAKRAS?

THIRD EYE CRYSTALS

The third eye is the physical energy center that manages our intuition and perspective. When it is open and optimally rotating, we are strongly connected to our knowledge of internal organs. It can be expressed by instincts, a spiritual vision, listening to messages, or merely knowing things.

The recognition of the guidance system, making better decisions, staying in the right place at the right time, and following the flow of life. However, there may be times when you need help opening and balancing the third eye chakra. That's where the Third Eye Crystal comes in.

The third eye crystal is a spiritual crystal that opens the third eye chakra. When carrying, holding, or bringing them to our energy sector, we can help awaken all the interests associated with the Third Eye.

The mental crystals associated with the third eye chakra tend to be purple, including amethyst, purple fluorspar, and sugilite. Other non-purple crystals of the third eye include obsidian, moldavite, lapis lazuli, and azurite.

CROWN CHAKRA CRYSTALS

The Crown Chakra is a physical energy center that manages connections to higher consciousness. It is how you connect with your guides, angels, and higher self. Crown chakra stones help us live from our values. They bring us strong empathy and selflessness and promote intelligence, wisdom, and psychological knowledge.

These crystals open the crown chakra and further improve communication with psychic and higher consciousness. By strengthening our spiritual connection, we experience more "chance."

These coincidences are merely spiritual guidance. You know what it looks like when something tells you to take another way home, and you will miss the accident. Everywhere you will see the same quote. Or meet an old friend in the industry you want to meet.

The crown chakra crystals you'll want to use are white like amethyst, clear quartz, rutile quartz, selenite, Herkimer diamonds, ametrine, and light.

WHY IS GROUNDING & PROTECTION IMPORTANT?

When we focus on spirituality, it is easy to lose ground, and this imbalance can cause physical and mental health problems. You can also deal with psychological attacks. It is where ground stones and protection stones come into play.

Some foundations are bronze, hematite, dragon stone, smoky quartz, garnet, and petrified wood.

The protective stones are mainly black, such as black tourmaline, obsidian, black onyx, and black jasper. Other are Firegate, Serpentine, Smoky Quartz, Labradorite, Red Jasper, and Moldavite. They act as a protective shield from negative energy and psychological attacks.

One of the best spiritual crystals is amethyst. It is a high-vibration pure crystal, but it also has durable protection so that you can get the benefits of both with one stone.

CONCLUSION

This book can help You to become aware of your chakras by paying attention to your mind-body-soul connection. Your body is continually changing, as are the state of your chakras, and it is up to you to bring awareness to your mind and body to detect any imbalances. Once you notice an imbalance, or if a particular part of your body doesn't feel quite right, you can turn to chakra healing crystals to help bring your body and your mind back to perfect balance.

COPYRIGHTS

This book

"CRYSTALS AND CHAKRAS FOR BEGINNERS: The Power of Crystals and Healing Stones! Discovering Crystals' Hidden Power! The Guide to Expand Mind Power, Enhance Psychic Awareness, Increasing your Spiritual Energy."

Written by Cassian Byrd

This Document aims to provide precise and reliable details on this subject and the problem under discussion.

The product has marketed on the assumption that no officially approved bookkeeping or publishing house provides other available funds.

Where a legal or qualified guide is required, a person must have the right to participate in the field.

A statement of principle, which is a subcommittee of the American Bar Association, a committee of publishers and Associations and approved. A copy, reproduction, or distribution of parts of this text, in electronic or written form, is not permitted.

The recording of this Document is strictly prohibited, and retention of this text is only with the written permission of the publisher and all Liberties authorized.

The information provided here is correct and reliable, as any lack of attention or other means resulting from the misuse or use of the procedures, procedures, or instructions contained therein is the total, and absolute obligation of the user addressed.

The author is not obliged, directly or indirectly, to assume civil or civil liability for any restoration, damage, or loss resulting from the data collected here. The respective authors retain all copyrights not kept by the publisher.

The information contained herein is solely and universally available for information purposes. The data is presented without a warranty or promise of any kind.

The trademarks used are without approval, and the patent is issued without the trademark owner's permission or protection.

The logos and labels here are the possessions of the owners themselves and are not associated with this text.

CPSIA information can be obtained
at www.ICGtesting.com
Printed in the USA
LVHW081018030721
691051LV00030B/835